Parenting
Sensibly

TURNING MESSES INTO SUCCESSES

A step by step guide which will help you navigate the imperfect parenting journey. It will strengthen relationships, reduce stress, and provide the tools you need to launch your children successfully into adulthood.

LYNDA SATRE

Move Mountains Publishing
Maryland, United States

Parenting Sensibly
Turning messes into successes

Scripture quotations marked (NIV) are taken from the Holy Bible, New International Version®, NIV®. Copyright © 1973, 1978, 1984, 2011 by Biblica, Inc.™ Used by permission of Zondervan. All rights reserved worldwide. www.zondervan.com The "NIV" and "New International Version" are trademarks registered in the United States Patent and Trademark Office by Biblica, Inc.™

Bulk purchase discounts available upon request by contacting publisher: parentingsensibly@gmail.com

Published by:
Move Mountains Publishing
Mounty Airy, Maryland, United States

Interior Design by: Jera Publishing
Book cover designed by JD&J with stock imagery provided by [Piotr Marcinski] © 123RF.com
Editing by: Morgan Feddes Satre & Kendra Juskus

Library of Congress Control Number: 2017912932

ISBN: 0-692-93881-8
ISBN: 978-0-692-93881-2

10 9 8 7 6 5 4 3 2 1

1. Parenting 2. Discipline of children 3. Child Rearing 4. Family Relationships

First Edition

Printed in the USA

Grateful
Thankful
Blessed

Dedicated to my soulmate, Dave. Thanks for
encouraging, believing in, and supporting me. There
is no one I'd rather do life with than you.

To my children: Each of you is an incredible blessing to me
and I love you, dearly. I am so thankful and proud to be your
mom. Thank you for your support and encouragement.

Thank you
so much!

I want to acknowledge my dear friends and family who have encouraged me through the huge task of writing this book, especially, Dawn, Neeta, Missy, Ariana, Angie, Josh, and Ben, who regularly checked up on my book's progress and encouraged me over the course of years.

Thank you, Morgan, my daughter-in-law, who not only read my raw manuscript and believed it needed to be published and shared, but who took on the task to edit and refine it into the book you have in your hands.

Thank you, Kendra Juskus, for your contribution and edits.

Thank you, Mom and Dad, for encouraging me and giving your blessing to publish this book.

Thank you to the many mentors I had on my parenting journey, through books, classes, and friendships. A special thanks to Mark Gregston, Bob Barnes, Kevin Leman, Gary Smalley, John Trent, Gary Chapman, Paula, Donley, Barb Tompkins, Cheryl Spessert, & Betty Chase. Thank you for the work you do to strengthen families.

Thanks be to God, who laid this book on my heart so long ago and surrounded me with people to encourage me to get this book written.

CONTENTS

INTRODUCTION

Why would I write a parenting book when there are so many other books already written? Visit your local bookstore, or do a search online, and you'll see that there are *a lot* of parenting books by experts on any topic you can imagine: personalities, potty-training, sleep, sibling rivalry, baby advice, parenting teens, boys, girls—the list goes on and on.

However, in all my own searching, I had a hard time finding a parenting book that was both comprehensive and practical—one that not only helped me see the big picture but also helped me with my everyday battles as a parent. So many parents are looking for the same thing. This book is what I wish had been available to me. Every chapter is designed to make both daily and long-term impacts.

I don't have the educational accolades that some authors do. But I do have the practical wisdom learned from raising 10 children over the past 26 years. Over time, I have learned many helpful lessons from books, parenting classes, and my own life experiences, all of which have been instrumental in my parenting direction. Now I want to pass those lessons on to you. I have already witnessed the incredible impact these lessons have on other families—this book is based on content I have used in parenting classes I've taught for the past five years.

You probably won't agree with everything I say; in fact, I expect that. Your background, your view of the world, and your own life experiences are different from mine. So look at this book like you do a grocery store.

When you're shopping, you buy the things you want and like; you leave behind the items you don't. Approach this book with the same mindset. Read it. Think about it. Apply those principles that stand out to you. Leave on the shelf those things that don't resonate with you, and keep reading the book until you find those points that do.

If I could, I would prefer to sit down with you one-on-one to chat about your life, your kids, your spouse or significant other, your hobbies, your dreams. I would like to just spend time together, your family and mine. But the reality is that likely won't happen. So when you read this book, picture each chapter as us sitting together over coffee, tea, or a tall glass of cold water, and eating my grandmother's melt-in-your-mouth molasses cookies. Take the kind of reflection you would do if I were there talking with you, and apply it as you read each chapter. What seemed to hit home for you? What stood out for you? There will be matters about which you say, "Yes, I am doing well in this area," and there will be areas you see the need to focus on and improve.

Some things I won't be able to address directly from experience. My views on this subject are shaped by my life experiences, and many of you are dealing with unique situations that differ greatly from mine. For example, I have not had to navigate parenting a child with physical or mental health challenges. Perhaps your relationship with your child is currently impacted by the loss of a parent, adoption, a significant family trauma, divorce, or any number of circumstances that need to be handled carefully. Though I believe this book will still be helpful to you, it may not fully assist you in your unique situation; in those instances, I recommend you consult a trained professional in addition to reading this book.

My parenting has also been deeply shaped by my faith perspective, and I want you to be aware of that. I am Christian, and I do talk about God in this book. Faith is foundational to my parenting, but I know the ideas in this book are applicable regardless of religious affiliation or non-affiliation. This book is meant to guide parents of all backgrounds, so I believe you can skim over anything that doesn't appeal to you and still find many useful nuggets to help you and your family.

Our family

I want to introduce you to me and my family. Not only will this help you better understand who's who in all the stories and examples I share, but it will also help you have a better idea of our family's background and how that has impacted my parenting.

My husband Dave and I met when we were in college in northeastern Iowa; I was a senior, and he was a junior. We were engaged the following summer and got married after Dave graduated from college. For the first few years of our marriage we lived in Iowa City while Dave attended graduate school and I worked full-time as a pediatric nurse. Our first son, Josh, was born 14 months after we were married. I worked 12-hour night shifts Friday, Saturday, and Sunday while Dave was home to care for Josh. It was a busy time with a lot of changes, but we did what we had to in order to make things work.

When Josh was 15 months old, Dave graduated, and we headed to Arizona to be closer to my family and begin his career. Our second son, Ben, was born just after Josh turned 2. After a while, we decided we would like to have another child, but that wasn't so easy. Thus began a heart-wrenching period of infertility. I had endometriosis laser surgery, tried infertility meds, and eventually we got certified to adopt. Going through the adoption certification process is a very humbling, stressful experience, not to mention adopting is expensive. But as we found out, once a couple is certified, actually being chosen to receive a baby is another long process. It was during this time that we decided to try a different infertility medication. Long story short, even though things didn't go as expected, God blessed us with fraternal twin boys, Sam and Nate. I was on bedrest for much of the pregnancy, but they were born healthy at 37 weeks when Josh and Ben were almost 4 and 6 years old.

Two years later, our fifth son, Jake, was born. When Jake was almost 2, Dave got promoted to a job in Washington state. With five young boys, we dreamed of a larger house with a lot of land where the kids to run and play. Given our budget, we knew it would have to be a fixer-upper. So we found a large 1970s rambler on three acres with lots of blackberries to pick and trees for a tree house. By that point, I was over 34 years old. Dave had listened for years to the possible complications of having kids past 35 and did not want more kids. We were buried in house projects, taking down brown paneling and replacing olive-green linoleum and orange countertops. Dave's job required extensive travel, and by then I was homeschooling the boys. Life was busy, and I was hoping my desire to have more kids would go away. Dave went ahead and had a vasectomy, while I prayed it wouldn't work. It did, and life, jobs, and homeschooling went on.

My desire for more kids just wouldn't go away. Dave didn't share my desire, so I prayed. Projects continued, and a couple of years went by. One day, after we had gone on a sightseeing day trip and were sitting at a sandwich shop, Dave said, "So, what should we do now?" I said, "I think we should have another baby." He said, "I was thinking along the lines of a vacation!"

By then, we had spent so many hours and numerous weekends on the house that I understood where he was coming from. However, this was the first time that I was fully able to express my heart and my desire to have more children. We looked into the cost of a vasectomy reversal, the odds of it working, and considered the reality that I was now 36 and had a history of infertility. Ultimately, Dave had the reversal surgery, and six months later, I was ecstatic to be pregnant. That was short-lived, however, because I miscarried soon after. Later that spring, we went on that much-needed vacation to Disney World. Upon our return from Florida, I found out I was pregnant again. We were blessed with our first daughter, Sophia, born more than five years after Jake.

The big surprise came when Sophia was still a baby—I got pregnant again. Sam, one of my fraternal twins, kept wondering if I was pregnant with twins. He had heard so many stories about when he and his twin were little that he wanted to "see" twins from another perspective. Even though he brought it up several times, I knew that I had had my first set of twins when I was on infertility meds and we had no family history of twins. So when we found out I *was* pregnant with twins, we were shocked. I came home and told Sam that God had heard his petition!

This twin pregnancy was a bit more complicated. They were identical twin boys, sharing one placenta. With Dave's frequent work travel schedule, I knew it would be difficult to care for twins, especially the night feedings. Fortunately, Dave secured a position at his company's corporate office that required less travel; unfortunately, it meant that I was 30 weeks pregnant when we moved from the Pacific Northwest to the East Coast. An Amtrak train was the only mode of transportation my doctors approved of for me to get across the United States. It was a 72-hour trip I am glad I don't have to repeat!

Two weeks after our arrival in our new home, Dave and I went to my doctor's appointment for a regular checkup. In the course of the appointment, we found out the twins were in distress because of Twin-to-Twin Transfusion Syndrome. Luke and Levi were born later that day via emergency C-section at 32 weeks. Sophia was 15 months old when they were born, but it was nearly another month before they were able to come home from the NICU.

I miscarried a baby when Luke and Levi were almost 2, but conceived our second daughter several months later. She had a twin, but her twin died early in the pregnancy. Katie is three years younger than Luke and Levi; I was 42 years old when she was born.

Our youngest son, Asher, was born 2.5 years later, when I was 44. I miscarried one more baby when I was 46. We are done having babies now. Our oldest sons are married and on their own, and we still have eight children at home. Ben, my second oldest son, and his wife will soon have their third child.

This is just a brief introduction to our family; as we journey throughout this book, you'll read stories that highlight the many personalities, talents, and dreams that each child has—as well as those more frustrating and painful moments that come from raising children.

This book stems from a large family with both parents, but I know the lessons in it are applicable to any parent—single or married, working or stay-at-home, mother or father. Though there is much about our parenting journey that I could talk about—the pain of infertility; the variations of childbirth; the pros and cons of public education, private education, homeschooling, community colleges, state universities, and private colleges (all of which our family has experienced); the merits of being a stay-at-home parent or a working parent—my focus in this book is to make a positive impact on you and your family through the parenting wisdom I have learned over the years. This knowledge has been life-changing for those who have taken my class, and I am confident it will help you as well.

My prayer for you is that through this book, you will find the joy and blessings of parenthood. I realize that the children in our lives may be planned, unplanned, adopted, step-children, your grandchildren, or the results of any number of circumstances. Regardless, the children in your life need YOU. Whether you feel like it or not, you are just the right person to guide and impact each child in your life. Parenthood is the toughest job you will have but also the most rewarding. I pray that in these chapters, you will find encouragement and helpful tips to strengthen your relationship with your children and your spouse or significant other. There is no race to read the book to the end; take time for reflection and implementation. In your career, your relationships, and your parenting, you didn't get to the place where you are overnight. It will be a process to make steps, one at a time, in another direction. Be encouraged. The fact you are reading this book shows your desire to improve things with your child. By the end of our journey together, I hope you can look back and see positive changes in your family.

Understanding Ourselves
and Our Children

Before we can begin the journey to better parent our children, we first need to look at ourselves. How and why do we parent the way we do? Understanding how we were raised and how we are currently raising our children will give us insight into the things we are doing well and the areas where we can improve. We will also go through how we compare ourselves to others, which can sometimes make us feel like parenting failures. Finally, we need to spend some time studying our children, so that we can have a deeper understanding of who they are and how we can connect with them.

CHAPTER 1

The Past Doesn't Determine
Your Future Parenting

 PARENTING POINT: Our past does affect us positively or negatively, but it does not determine our future

Every person has their own style and beliefs about raising their children. There are many factors that go into developing these convictions, but one of the biggest is how you were parented. You may parent just like your parents; maybe you do the opposite. Either way, it is important to take some time to reflect on the parenting style your parents used and realize how it has affected your own parenting. If you are following in the footsteps of great parents, then you are starting with a good foundation. And if you realize you're using some—or all—of the same parenting techniques that were harmful to you as a child, remember: You have a choice. It will require you to stop, think, and intentionally choose to parent differently, but you *can* change.

Some of us come from homes with strict parents who had the "You Better Obey or Else" philosophy. Some of us come from homes where parents used very little discipline or structure in raising us and acted more as a friend than a parent. Some of us come from loving, balanced homes. Some of us, for one reason or another, had very little parental involvement, whether it was because we were home alone or our parents were so emotionally distant it was like they weren't there, even if they were physically in the room. And unfortunately, some of us have come from abusive homes.

No matter our background, how we were raised affects us—sometimes positively, sometimes negatively. Oftentimes, it's a bit of both. We may have deep-seated resentment toward our parents; we may be extremely grateful for them. Some find ourselves parenting just like our parents did—even if we don't want to—because that is the only way we know. Some of us go to the extreme opposite of our parents. To complicate things even further, our spouse or significant other has their own background and parenting philosophy, which may or may not be in line with our own.

My Search for Parenting Guidance

When Dave and I were new parents living in Tucson, Arizona, I sought classes for guidance in parenting. Having two young boys, I wanted so much to parent well, but I really didn't know what that looked like. I took several classes at different churches, but I didn't find anything that proved very helpful until my friend told me about the Mom's Class[1] at a church across town. She had taken the class the year before and couldn't talk highly enough about it.

So off I went to the Mom's Class; it didn't take long for me to understand why my friend had loved it so much. It was the first time I had weekly practical help that was applicable in my own home. In a short amount of time, I saw significant changes in the atmosphere of my home, and I felt better equipped because I had some tools and direction. I couldn't finish out the class because of having to be on bedrest due to preterm labor during my first twin pregnancy, but even in an abbreviated format, that class stuck with me.

Over the course of the following years, I continued taking other parenting classes and read dozens of parenting books. Why was I searching so hard? I started my parenting journey with some baggage—particularly in my relationship with my father. A key part of my parenting journey was reflecting on my father's journey to becoming a parent to me.

Looking Beyond the Past

In order to understand why my father parented the way he did, I had to look at how *he* was parented as a child—or rather, how he wasn't parented.

My father's parents both drank too much, which led to employment and financial challenges. My father had an older half-sister and half-brother, and he was the oldest of the next six children born. When he was 15, his parents wanted him to quit school to start working at a factory. It just seemed logical to them. He really wanted to finish high school, because he knew that was the only way to get ahead. Fortunately, even though his parents were both Canadian, he happened to be born in Michigan where his dad was working illegally. (A few months after he was born, they moved back to Canada where they remained the rest of their lives.) So he left home at 15 carrying a small paper sack that held all he owned, crossed into the United States, and went to live with his aunt and uncle in Minnesota, who were childless and lived in a one-bedroom house. My dad lived there, sleeping on the couch, until he was 16 and could rent a room at the YMCA.

My father ended up being on his own at 16, supporting himself by working at a grocery store, where he eventually became a manager. After a time, he became the owner of two auto parts stores, which is how he supported our family for the first 18 years of my life. For my dad, this was a sign of his good parenting—he was providing financial stability for us, which was something his own parents struggled to accomplish. We had a middle-class house, clothes, and food, and we took a vacation in our station wagon once a year.

Unfortunately, my father drank as well, though in a less obvious way than his father had. He would stop at the bar on his way home from work and drink with his buddies. However, when he drank, he said and did things that were hurtful. As a child, I did not understand—and certainly did not process—how the alcohol caused him to do these things. When I was younger, I learned to avoid him; when I got older, I often confronted him and accepted the consequences. As a result, our relationship was extremely strained.

When I was in ninth grade, we had a house fire that was started in the clothes dryer. Although no one was hurt, the damage to our home was extensive, and we couldn't live there for a few months because of the toxic fumes and fire damage. Our insurance only paid the depreciated value, not the replacement value of the damaged items, so my dad was stressed about our finances.

For my birthday that year, I asked for a phone for my room—one of those old corded dial phones available in 1982. I also needed a new bed since mine had been ruined in the fire, and I requested a water bed. My father got very angry and said, "I wish you had never been born!"

Ouch.

What I didn't know at the time was that he had been drinking; he never remembered saying those words. Yet they haunted me for many years and sent me down a detrimental path. Though my father went through an amazing transformation that led to a reconciliation in our relationship and healing for both of us (which you can read more about in Chapter 17), the impact of those words changed my life. And they changed my parenting.

Each of you has a story—your story. Your parents do, too, which affected how they raised you. However, the good news is that though the past affects you, it does *not* determine your future. Dysfunction can be passed from generation to generation, but it doesn't *have* to be. That cycle can be broken, and new pathways can be taken. We can reject harmful cycles of poor parenting and instead work to pass on positive multigenerational patterns through our examples to our children.

That realization was what led me to attend numerous parenting classes and read countless books. I wanted to break the cycle. I deeply desired to have a better relationship with my children than I had with my dad. I didn't want my kids to experience the hurt I had felt. I didn't want them to experience the fear I had when my dad was angry. I didn't want them to feel worthless, like I had.

Through parenting classes, books, and mentors, I started to figure out what kind of parent I wanted to become. I wanted to become an authoritative parent.

Four Types of Parenting

There are two key aspects foundational to parenting: love and discipline. Children need to know they are loved; they also need boundaries and discipline in order to learn and grow.

Various combinations of these aspects create four unique parenting styles, illustrated in the figure below:

PARENTING STYLES[2]

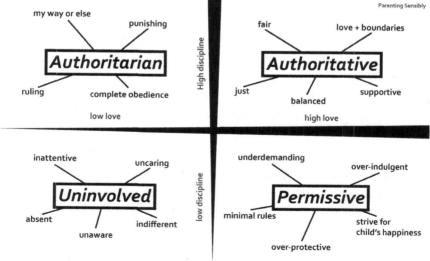

To understand this chart, think of the two foundational aspects of parenting as each having their own scale ranging from low to high. The horizontal line represents the amount of parental love that is visible and recognizable by the children, with low levels of love on the left and high levels on the right. (Note that while parents may truly hold minimal love toward their children, this scale generally refers to what is *visible* to the children, which may not always accurately reflect how the parent truly loves and cares about their child. We will discuss how to better show our love as parents to meet each child's unique needs in Chapter 4.)

The vertical line measures the amount of discipline used by parents, with low levels at the bottom and high levels at the top. (We will discuss what healthy discipline looks like in Section 2.)

Now, depending on how much love and discipline is utilized by a parent, that parent's style will fall generally into one of four main categories:

AUTHORITARIAN – Parents who use a lot of discipline but do not show a lot of love.

UNINVOLVED – Parents who use little discipline but also show little love.

PERMISSIVE – Parents who do not use much discipline but show a lot of love.

AUTHORITATIVE – Parents who use a lot of healthy discipline in raising their children but also show a lot of love to their children.

The diagram offers a number of descriptor words that offer different insights into each parenting style. This book will teach how to become an authoritative parent, fostering a home that balances both love and discipline. Below are general examples of the different parenting styles. Within each category there is a continuum, from a little bit to the extreme. Each family is unique and can't always perfectly fit into one box, but you will be able to see a bent or tendency reflected in your own parenting style.

Authoritarian

This parent is quick and heavy on the discipline. Often the children are seen but not heard. "Obey or else" is a common attitude these parents have. Usually there are plenty of rules, but often love is not shown as clearly. On the extreme end, these parents can fall into physical or emotional abuse.

Uninvolved

On the extreme, this parent is physically and/or emotionally absent, leaving a child unattended, left to fend for himself. However, there are other parents who are physically present, but still not engaged either physically or emotionally. This can seem to the child that the parent is detached or distant; the parent has their life, and children are left to themselves to make their way through life. This child does not feel the parent's love and is also lacking boundaries and guidance.

Permissive

This parent is affectionate, showering her child with love. However, there are few rules, and the rules that do exist are not consistently enforced. This parent wants to do everything they can for their child and protect them. Keeping her child happy is a top priority. This parent can sometimes fall into being a "helicopter" parent.

Authoritative

This parent has clear boundaries but is also warm and affectionate. The parent is actively engaged with the children, playing games, assisting with homework when needed, and attending their sporting or school activities. The parent has rules and disciplines when necessary, but also makes sure their kids know they love them.

Reflecting on Painful Memories

For some of you, I have opened up a huge can of worms and have brought to mind deep wounds, pain, and memories you would rather keep pushed down. This is something I do not take lightly; reflecting on my own past has often been painful. But processing these feelings and memories is a vital first step to moving forward into a healthier style of parenting.

You and I are not alone in this struggle. Here is what a dear friend who took my first class wrote:

> When I stepped into Lynda's parenting class for the first time, I knew I needed help with parenting. The perfectionist in me was excited to learn from someone wiser how to "do it right." But what I didn't realize was that in order to take this journey forward, I was going to have to go back and look at how I was parented as a child. That was hard. I didn't sign up for that. That was a part of my life I had spent years trying to keep closed off, shut down, and pushed to the back corners of my mind. Many times, just thinking about it had me well up with tears of shame, or I would get sweaty with fear and anxiety. The voices of the enemy whispered (or often shouted) that things would never be different, it was too late, and that I could never change. And for many years, I believed that voice. For so long, I let fear of my past cloud my vision for my future. But God. On the day this very chart was projected onto the screen in the front of the room, and tears began to well up once again and the fear and self-doubt loomed over me like a heavy cloak, I scribbled these words down on the paper in front of me:

I am deeply loved.

I am fully forgiven.

I am completely accepted.

It took everything I had in me not to walk out of the room.

Grieving my childhood has been one of the most difficult parts of motherhood. As I learned new and different ways to approach raising my children, I was forced to grieve what was and was not provided for me in my own life. If, as you read, you too may find your definition of "normal" being shattered by the wisdom of this book. I encourage you to press on. Press on toward the goal of having a beautiful family.

Around the time I was in Lynda's class, I attended a Matthew West concert, and the lyrics of "Family Tree" left me in a puddle in my seat. Now, just a few short years later, having watched Him break the chains of abuse, abortion, affairs, and alcoholism, I am confident that He who began a good work in me will carry it on to completion until the day of Christ. And that promise is NOT just for me. Sister/ Brother, may I encourage you to believe that that promise is for you and your family as well!

I highly recommend for you to listen and watch Matthew West's song, "Family Tree."[3] It sums up this chapter. No one chooses to be born into a dysfunctional family and it isn't your fault if that was your history. The good news is that you can completely change the course for *your* family and break the cycle of dysfunction. It isn't always going to be easy, but take one step at a time and one day you will look back and see how far you have come.

I am hoping to show you how to become an authoritative parent. Love *and* discipline are needed—not one more than another, but in equal doses. This book will go through what this looks like. Parenting is a journey. You didn't get to the place you are overnight, and it will take time to implement changes. It will be helpful for you to think, journal, and write down what you want to work on each week. Changes will come over time.

1. What were your parents' parenting styles?
2. What is your parenting style?
3. What is your significant other's parenting style?
4. Write down what you would like to change in your family.

CHAPTER 2

The Perfect Parent: The Lie We Have Believed

 PARENTING POINT: There is no perfect parent, family, or child

We had been on the road, living out of a suitcase for almost six weeks, and the kids were out-of-sorts. Our hotel was by a mall, so we often ate at the food court. Being new to a city, alone with four young children, I would scour the newspaper in search of something to do. That day, we went to the park to attend an event I had discovered in the paper; by the time we got lunch, it was late, and the kids were very hungry and crabby. They couldn't agree on which food they wanted, so I had to go to different food court vendors for the various meals, which included waiting for a cheese pizza to be made. I finally got all the kids seated with food, and one son promptly spilled an entire glass of pop (soda, for those of you who are not from the Midwest). I was totally at the end of my rope. I did what I could to remain calm, but I was crumbling.

Haven't we all felt this way when things were not going as we had hoped? I, too, have days when I am overwhelmed and unequipped. I am not perfect, and neither are my husband or children. Parenting is hard, and there are many challenges along the way. There is no one perfect way to parent, and there are no perfect families, but there are things that I have found very helpful in navigating this imperfect, but wonderful, parenting journey.

The Power of a Sympathetic Ear

When my fifth son, Jake, was an infant, my twins, Sam and Nate, were 2 years old. Nate has always been my "Tigger," going through life bouncing and jumping; he's impulsive and likes to get a laugh. Fortunately for him—and unfortunately for me—Sam found this very amusing. So whenever I heard laughter, I knew there was trouble.

Once, they threw a dozen eggs around my kitchen and family room. Another day, they splatted an entire large tub of margarine around my family room, covering the walls, windows, leather couches, and floor. During a time-out, they emptied their entire dresser of clothes and heaped them on their little toddler beds. I told them to put all the clothes back; they pulled out the bottom drawer and stuffed them all inside.

Sam and Nate at 2; Margarine covering my family room; Clothes all put away, mom!

I couldn't believe that my children would do such things; my friends' kids hadn't, nor had my older two sons. Dave received many phone calls with me in tears. He would try to "fix" things, but what I really wanted was for someone to listen to my frustration and empathize. I found it so helpful to call other moms of twins who would share their own stories and help me feel that I wasn't alone.

I also found tremendous help from the encouragement of strangers. That day in the food court, with crabby kids and spilled pop, feeling embarrassed and exhausted, I was at my wit's end. As I cleaned up the mess, two ladies came over to me and said, "I just wanted you to know that you are doing a very good job in the midst of the situation."

Wow! That made a *huge* impact on my day. When things were not going well, just to have someone give me encouragement instead of stares and judgment was a blessed relief.

The Danger of Comparison

It is so easy to look at parents who appear to have it all together and have "perfect" children and to feel yourself inadequate. When someone is bragging about how their 18-month-old was potty-trained in a day, it makes those of us with a child almost 4 and not yet fully potty-trained feel completely incompetent.

With today's technology, the lure of comparison is stronger than ever before. Seeing pictures of elaborate birthday parties or hearing about another child's latest glowing achievement can be a blow to your parenting self-esteem. But we must remember that few people take pictures of their kid's meltdowns at a store or poor report cards. They only show a glimpse of the "best." Trust me—real life is not as perfect as it appears.

In fact, I'm convinced that many developmental achievements have nothing to do with parental expertise; much depends on the unique characteristics of each child. I have children who were early, fluent readers and others who found reading to be slow and laborious. I had early talkers and a child who needed to go to speech therapy for a year.

I had children who walked early and another one who didn't walk until he was 15 months old.

Each of my children is unique; that's part of why I love them so deeply. That's also part of what makes parenting so challenging. I am not to blame for the children who struggled with reading, the one who was late to walk, or those who were late to talk; nor can I take credit for those who mastered things early. It wasn't something I did or didn't do. I think the parents who happen to have a baby who slept through the night at four weeks or had a child who potty-trained easily could be just lucky. We, as parents, really don't have that much power! Don't get me wrong, parents influence their children, but each child is unique—even children within the same family.

We also need to stop thinking we need to do everything everyone else does. Years ago, I was talking with a friend who had recently returned from visiting her grandkids. Her daughter's husband was out of town for work; her daughter needed her to come because she and her nanny couldn't do everything alone for the two children. There was the twice-a-week foreign language class, twice-a-week swimming, gymnastics, and of course music class—and that wasn't everything. The age of her grandkids? Three years old and 11 months! When asked why she didn't just pick one or two activities for her kids, the mother said, "I have to expose them to everything so we can figure out what they are good at—and besides, everyone is doing this." She didn't want her children to be behind. This was all done in an effort to be a "perfect parent." But there was little time for bike rides or walks; the children had no idea how to play on their own.

The Importance of Context

I know we have all had those dreadful parenting moments when we wished we could have disappeared. It is embarrassing, and it feels like the eyes of disapproval and judgment are crushing.

It is just as easy to look at parents who have a child throwing a fit, a pregnant teen, or a teen struggling with drugs or alcohol, and see them as parenting failures. However, you have no idea what the background of the situation is. Maybe that child throwing the fit was extremely tired from having to get up early to get to daycare that morning. Maybe the parents of those teens tried everything to reach out to their children, but those children chose a different path. This world would be a lot better if there was less judging and more kindness and compassion given.

Kindness and compassion were given to me that day at the food court. And boy, was there a backstory behind my exhaustion and my children's crabbiness. We had been living in Arizona when Dave got a job transfer to the Seattle area. I had thought it was too hard to keep the house perfect for showing while we were living there, with five young boys and white tile throughout much of the house, so I thought it would be easier to spend a few weeks at my in-laws in Minnesota.

We loaded up the five boys in the van and headed north to spend several weeks in Minnesota. It was *hot* in Arizona in May, and I hadn't planned on Minnesota's highs only being in the 40s. I was totally unprepared. All we had to wear were shorts, and it certainly wasn't fun to go and do anything outside, especially without warm clothes. It was a rough few weeks.

In June, we headed to Seattle. Another very long car ride ended with Dave dropping us off at a hotel in our new town as he traveled to San Francisco for a 10-day work trip. I found myself with four young sons (one of my sons stayed with my in-laws for a special trip they do when each of my kids is 7 years old) in a city I didn't know. We had to eat out for all our meals, find something to do during the day, and somehow all sleep in our one hotel room. By this time, we had been gone from our home in Tucson for almost six weeks, and the kids were tired of being on the road and living out of a suitcase.

That was how I ended up in the food court with crabby kids and spilled pop. And that is why the encouragement those two women gave me was so life-giving. They could have assumed many things in that moment; instead, they chose to give me a word of encouragement. It was a small thing for them, but it was a big deal to me. When you witness another parent struggling, please step out and be that life-giving encourager! Your positive words may make more of a difference than you can imagine.

Not long ago, I read a story about a mom in Australia who was eating at a restaurant when her 8-week-old son started fussing, wanting to eat. Shortly after she started nursing her son, an older woman walked over to her. The mother braced herself for criticism; instead, the woman encouraged this new mom and started cutting up her food for her so she could eat before it got cold. This random act of kindness made international news![4]

The bottom line is, if you see a mom in the parking lot struggling to push her cart while carrying a screaming kid, lend a hand with the cart. If you see a mom near tears in public, let her know that you've had days like that, too, and see how you can help. When you see someone who could use an ear, a meal, or encouragement, don't just think about it—do it. Let's start a movement of showing encouragement to those around us. Small acts of kindness make huge impacts!

Parenting Doesn't Have a Perfect Formula

I have known some amazing parents over the years who have had a child who struggled with drugs, alcohol, or depression. These parents worked very hard to raise their children with a good balance of love and discipline, and they felt pain and sadness as they watched their children struggle. Children do grow up and make their own choices, and not all of them are good. There are many instances where it is easy to understand why a young adult is struggling; there are also many instances where it is not. Perhaps a teen's poor choices—not any fault of a parent—led them down the wrong path. Perhaps an underlying mental illness was the cause. Any number of unknown factors could be at play; it is not our place to judge. Instead, we need to offer grace and support to families in need.

There are unexplainable outcomes of parenting in the other direction, too. I have heard many stories about the horrific abuse some people have endured in childhood, and I am shocked at how well those individuals have overcome their past to become stable adults. Through the help of mentors and others along the way, these people have been able to beat the odds and find success and stability as adults.

If you see a family that looks perfect, you probably aren't seeing the whole picture. So many people are shocked when a celebrity couple who had a seemingly perfect relationship gets a divorce. The problems were there, but they didn't let the public see them. There are no such things as perfect parents, perfect kids, or perfect families.

As frustrating as this may be to hear, there isn't a perfect parenting formula with a 100 percent guarantee. But there are ways to parent that have been shown to be more helpful in the long-run. I don't claim to be a perfect parent with perfect children, but I have learned a lot on my parenting journey. I believe the principles I am sharing with you will positively influence your family and help immensely as you navigate the ups and downs of parenting.

1. How do you compare yourself with other parents?
2. Do you do things not because you want to but because others are doing them?
3. Decide that from now on, you are going to stop judging others and stop putting unrealistic expectations on yourself.
4. Start making decisions for your family based solely on what is in the best interest of your family.

CHAPTER 3

Embracing the Uniqueness
of Each Child

PARENTING POINT: "Many family conflicts are caused by viewing another person's natural strengths as weaknesses." Trent & Smalley

Several years ago, my son Nate used a steak knife to peel an orange. When his bowl was filled with orange peels, he got up from the couch to throw them away and then—true to Nate's style—decided to do a flip over the back of the couch to sit down and eat his snack. Unbeknownst to everyone, the knife that he had used was still on the couch and perched in just the right position so that when he performed his acrobatic feat, the knife lodged about 2.5 inches into his buttocks.

At the time, I was in the kitchen. I saw him doing an odd jumping dance and asked him what was going on. When I came around the corner, all I could see was a slice in his jeans and blood pouring out; the moment after it had happened, Nate had seen the knife sticking through his jeans and had rapidly ripped it out.

I spent many years training to become and then working as a nurse; blood was not new to me. But as I assessed the wound, I knew I had never hoped to see that deep into tissue outside a medical facility, so yet another trip to the ER was in order—one of many with Nate.

Trips to the ER with Nate are not unusual. In fact, we have had more injury-related ER trips with Nate than any other child. He races through life having fun and taking risks. We have other children who are much more cautious and have had far fewer injuries. Though I could have tolerated fewer trips to the ER, I am so thankful to have Nate and his personality in my life. He makes life more fun, spontaneous, and interesting.

Each one of our children is unique. We need a world like that: including all kinds of people with all kinds of personalities and strengths. Could you imagine a world filled with people who had the same personality, strengths, and weaknesses? That would not work well at all.

I am sure you see differences among members of your own family, as well as among members of the family you grew up in. Each personality has positive and negative qualities. However, there isn't a "bad" personality. We need them all. Learning to recognize and embrace each child as the unique person God created will go a long way in making your child feel accepted.

We must also remember that our kids are not the only ones with different personalities; we are unique, as well. Our personality influences the way we tend to parent. I have already discussed the need for both love *and* discipline. We shouldn't parent with only one or the other; there needs to be balance between them. This is how we become authoritative parents who both love and discipline their children. *How* we get to that point, however, will look different depending on both our personalities and our children's personalities. Throughout this chapter, think about your personality and how that influences your relationships, as well as ways you can improve the balance between love and discipline.

There are countless personality profiles, acronyms, studies, and names for each personality type. For our purposes, I am going to follow the model that Gary Smalley and John Trent use in their book, *The Two Sides of Love:*[5] I will discuss personalities in terms of animal names, because I find them easy to picture and remember. I recommend reading *The Two Sides of Love* to delve much deeper into this topic. The four animals used to describe personalities in this method are otter, lion, beaver, and golden retriever. We have some of each personality in our family; you probably do, too!

OTTER. Nate, the son whose stabbed himself in his bottom, is one of our otters. "It will all work out," is a motto he lives by. In our family's experience, the otters have our best family stories. They are the life of the party; fun is just waiting to happen with an otter in your life.

On another occasion, Nate was practicing backflips on our neighbor's trampoline. He thought it was a good idea to do half-flips, where he would flip and land on his hands. My son Jake encouraged him: "Go really high this time!" (Otters are very susceptible to peer pressure.) When Nate did so and came down on his hands, both bones in his left forearm snapped upon impact. All the boys heard the break, and Nate watched the bones move in a way that they shouldn't. He ran home, holding his arm, plopped down on the couch, and said, "I definitely broke my arm."

At the time, I was making dinner, and my brother, his wife, and their three boys had just arrived from Arizona the night before for their first visit to our home on the East Coast. I had to leave them in charge of everyone and dinner while I headed to the ER. On the way to the hospital, Nate continually and calmly repeated, "It really hurts, Mom. I saw on *Mythbusters* that it doesn't help your pain to yell or scream." He talked about his pain in a calm manner, but he looked like he was ready to pass out.

Nate had broken the same bones in the same arm at age 6 when he dropped from monkey bars. After he got his cast off that time, his doctor told him he couldn't jump or run for another month—an impossible request with a kid like Nate!

Nate's first broken arm at 6.

Nate's 2ⁿᵈ broken arm at 14!

In addition to his energetic, daredevil nature, Nate is a constant prankster. Several years ago, he hid himself, waiting to jump out and scare his brother as he walked out of the bathroom. All went according to plan, except for one detail: It was Grandma, not his brother, who came out of the bathroom! The tables turned on that one; we are the ones who laugh about that now.

Katie's interesting outfit at 4

Katie is our other otter, and she proves that these personalities are evident even as infants. Once, we went out for dinner when Katie was only 4 months old. From her high chair, she cooed and smiled at the women in the next booth, and every time they looked away from her, she would vocalize to get their attention again!

As Katie grows older, she continues to talk and engage with anyone who will listen. She loves to be around people, and they love to be around her. However, sometimes, when it comes to getting work done, she will either "forget," ignore her assigned task, or come up with something else she would rather do. When she was young, it was not uncommon for her to have mismatched socks or shoes without a care in the world about it. The important part was that she had something on; matching was not that big of a deal. She tells very detailed and animated stories, with a tendency to interrupt others in her excitement, but ultimately a capacity to make friends with anyone.

Katie's ever-present smile since infancy

The **OTTER** *PARENT* is often a hugging, laughing, and fun parent. My friends who are otter parents are extremely fun to be around. They are the ones who call me up and invite me to meet them at the park, go to the apple orchard, or join in other various activities. They love to get into the sand with their kids, building sandcastles and moats. While doing art activities with preschoolers is a blast for an otter parent, it is totally stressful for beavers like me who can only focus on how much time it is going to take to clean up the mess! However, otter parents can have a hard time saying "no" to their children; they would rather have fun and be a friend than have boundaries and discipline. So they can fall into being a permissive parent: strong in love, but lacking in discipline.

LION. Lions are the natural-born leaders who like to accomplish things with immediate results—*now*! They are decisive and feel threatened when questioned. Many children labeled as "strong-willed children" have the lion personality. We have a couple of lions in our house, and sometimes the claws come out, figuratively speaking (well, mostly figuratively).

Lions like to be in control and delegate work—a trait that isn't always welcomed by siblings! They can be stubborn and often have a hard time

Jake did headstand for 13 mins.

*Jake determined to set a
family headstand record*

admitting they are wrong. Josh and Jake (my first and fifth sons) are both lions. Josh has always had clear direction and a strong work ethic. He also views things as black-and-white, right-and-wrong, with not a lot of gray area. For example, when Josh was a 3-year-old at preschool, his teacher would say things like, "If you keep jumping, you are going to fall through the floor," to children who were jumping around, or "If you keep doing that, your hair is going to fall out," to children who shook their heads back and forth. Josh would come home just livid at those comments. In his view, you speak the truth, and that is that!

Josh also would never take "no" for an answer; instead, he would think of all the reasons why we should say "yes." When he was a preschooler, we used to joke that he would make a good lawyer. Now that he's an adult, the funny thing is that he actually would go to law school if it didn't cost so much!

Josh was a very direct, intense child, which is common with fast-paced, decisive lion personalities. He wasn't one to sit down and self-entertain. Even at a few months old, he was happiest when I read to him. As a preschooler, every day he would ask, "What are we going to do today?" I would tell him, then he would say, "What next? And after that?" He also enjoys being on the go all day long.

Shortly after we moved to Tucson, Arizona, we went to a huge outdoor desert museum called the Sonora Desert Museum. Josh had not been walking for very long at that point, but he was very verbal. I wanted to take a stroller, and he would have nothing to do with it. I told him that if we did not take the stroller, he would have to walk the whole time—we wouldn't carry him. That is exactly what he did, and he never complained once. So it has come as no surprise to us that his best swimming event was the mile and that he completed two marathons before turning 25!

Parenting a lion can be exhausting, as there are often constant debates and struggles for control. A lion wants to be in charge, and they don't like to be questioned or admit they are wrong. Oftentimes, others don't want to be under that leadership, though lions do tend to be very successful CEOs. At 2 years old, Jake, our other lion, would direct his older brothers in exactly what they would play each day. He has made up numerous games over the years; of course, if you make up the game, you make up the rules, which can certainly be in your favor!

Josh after completing a marathon

Jake is also competitive and always keeping up with Sam and Nate, who are two years older. So when his big brothers were doing school, Jake was right there learning alongside them. Not surprisingly, when Sam and Nate started taking classes at the community college at 17, Jake applied and went, too, at 15.

The **LION *PARENT*** sets high goals for themselves and their kids. Some expect complete obedience, and when that doesn't happen, the discipline usually comes swiftly and with little explanation. Phrases that are often uttered by lion parents include, "As long as you live under my roof, you will do things my way," and, "You will do as I say and that's that."

The lion parent can view questions or discussion as disrespect. That was certainly the case with my father, who has this personality. The child in this home can feel hurt and angry. The challenge for this parent is to work on giving more positive affirmation to their child so the relationship can be strengthened. It is also important for lion parents to learn to relax and develop humility. This parent tends to be strong in discipline but usually needs to work on showing love. "Lions can be so strong that they win every verbal battle but end up losing the war for their family's hearts."[6]

BEAVER. A beaver has a perfectionist, analytical, soft-spoken temperament. A beaver is a good problem solver and likes order and schedules; the "busy beaver" description is certainly apt. Beavers actually *read* instructions, make careful decisions, and use critical skills to solve problems. They live by the motto, "Let's do it right."

Sam, Sophia, Luke, and Levi are beavers. What I appreciate about Sam is his attention to detail. He is the one who always makes sure the younger kids have their shoes on and tied, coats on, and car seats buckled. His school work is neat and orderly. When we are doing yardwork or a building project, he works hard until the project is done. He is responsible; as a young teen, he started mowing lawns and shoveling snow for neighbors, creating an organized system along the way. His hard work ethic, dependability, and conscientiousness make him a very responsible person, but he also is easily emotionally hurt and can be critical of others.

Sophia is also very responsible. At twelve, she is a great help at home and also volunteers at church. She has helped her younger siblings for years through such activities as making lunches and doing her little sister's hair. She loved to help me in the kitchen when she was young, and now she bakes and cooks on her own.

Sophia helping when young; As a pre-teen she is baking independently

Luke and Levi like order and cleanliness. I never have to remind them to wash their hands, and often they are the ones who request hand sanitizer when we are in public. They keep their rooms the cleanest of all my children.

If your child is a beaver, it is important to help your child understand that it is okay to fail and ask for help when struggling. Beavers are more likely to internalize failure and blame themselves, which can lead to depression. It is also important to be aware of their sensitivity to criticism.

The **BEAVER** *PARENTS* are focused on making their children turn out "right." They want their children to learn responsibility and strive for excellence. They are

Sam taking care of Asher

detail-oriented and are great at planning, setting schedules, or arranging what is needed to keep things organized. They like to explain their reasons for everything; this means that at times, they might provide too many details or appear to be lecturing others. This type of parent is at risk for being a perfectionist. It is important for this parent to work on relationships more and emphasize performance less. This parent tends

to be good at discipline but needs to be attentive to showing love and maintaining close relationship. Like with all parents, it is important to strive for that balance between love and discipline found in the authoritative parenting style.

Both my mother-in-law and I are beavers. For

My clean and orderly duo

beavers, the importance of details can make others feel judged and feel like they can't measure up. One of the *weaknesses* of a beaver is that it is very hard to take criticism, and we also focus on the past. So, if my mother-in-law commented on how I did something, it made me feel hurt. But by understanding more about different personalities—including my own—I am better able to understand that she isn't trying to be critical; instead, that is part of how her personality leads her to express herself, and I must not take it so personally. As a beaver parent, it is so important for your kids to hear positive affirmation from you and for you to work on your relationship with them, showing love and tenderness.

GOLDEN RETRIEVER. A warm, affectionate, easy-going golden retriever is quite pleasant to be around. They are loyal, have a strong need for close relationships, have a deep need to please others, have hearts full of compassion, and adapt to new environments. However, they don't like sudden changes and hold stubbornly to what they feel is right.

Ben is one of our golden retrievers. He has always been a go-with-the-flow kid. As a child, Ben was always happy to do whatever; he would fall asleep instantly in the car and then wake up cheerfully when we got to our destination. He easily made friends at the park or wherever we were; of course, he usually didn't know his new friend's name, but nevertheless he happily played until it was time to leave.

The **GOLDEN RETRIEVER** *PARENT* is a warm, affectionate parent who nurtures and meets the family's needs. They are calm and like to serve, and

Ben, a peacemaker with animals and people

they model good family routines and traditions. However, this kind of parent can fall into being a "helicopter parent" who wants to swoop in and protect their children from teachers, playmates, or anything perceived as hostile. They also can allow others to walk all over them and may struggle with not feeling appreciated. This parent tends to be good at showing love, but needs to focus on being consistent with discipline.

When Nate had his knife mishap, I made my SOS call to my husband Dave. Dave, being a calm golden retriever, told me to have Josh and Ben, my oldest two sons, drop Nate off at the ER on their way to swim team practice. He would be at the ER to meet them since he worked across the street from the hospital. That way, I could get the other kids to their swim practice, which was 30 minutes in the other direction. It was unnerving for me, the beaver, to send a son with a stab wound with his teenage brothers to the ER, but Dave was completely calm and methodical, and it worked out well.

Dave is easy to be married to because he hates conflict! A golden retriever is a peacemaker, a good listener, stable, personable, and loyal. I especially appreciate Dave's loyalty to our family, our marriage, his work, and his faith. Because of his desire to love and please, it is sometimes harder for him to discipline and stay firm on the rules, especially when they are upsetting to the kids. Because of this loyalty, adaptability, and deep need to please others, golden retrievers can fall into a codependency role and end up in unhealthy relationship situations. Also, "the same compassionate heart that can spot the hurt of others can be easily hurt by others as well."[7]

There are billions of people in this world, and God created each one individually, with unique personalities, histories, and quirks. It is not easy to put everyone into four categories, even categories as broad as these, but finding the exact label of your child's personality is not the main point of this exercise. Instead, I simply want you to study your children. Get to know their uniqueness. What gifts do they have? What are their passions? What makes them happy and what upsets them? What is your personality, and how does that affect how you relate to your child?

Understanding your children's individual personalities will help you think about each of them in a different light. This isn't to excuse misbehavior or say, "Well, that's just the way he is." But it hopefully will help you understand your child better. There are many different personalities in each home; each one needs to feel that they are an important part of that family and that they are loved and accepted for who they are.

For further study on this topic, in addition to *The Two Sides of Love* by Gary Smalley and John Trent, I also recommend the book, *Different*

Children, Different Needs, by Dr. Charles Boyd.[8] It provides examples of each of the different personalities (although it uses different terms) and what each personality looks like as a child or as a parent. It also gives examples about people in the Bible who had that personality and how God models each parenting style.

I cannot emphasize enough how important it is to understand your children's personalities. Some personalities live together more harmoniously than others, but regardless, we need to know our children and love them in a way they feel accepted and like they fit into the family. This means we can't parent each child the same; we have to adjust according to what each child *needs*. We need to be able to understand the ins and outs of each child, to enhance their strengths, and work on areas they struggle in. Being "fair" and treating each person exactly the same is not how we should address parenting. The parent needs to be able to flex with each child and personality, as well as with their different ages and stages.

However, understanding our children's personalities is only one part of the equation. We need to open our hearts and eyes to understand our own personalities so we can see ourselves as we are—both the good and the bad. It is only through seeing the truth that we can begin to recognize areas where we need to change. This will help us see our children as the unique gifts God created. Our goal is to nurture, discipline, and train them in such a way that they can feel our love and acceptance. We need to view their strengths for what they are, and not as weaknesses, and we need to strive to grow closer in our relationships during this parenting journey.

1. Spend time studying your own personality with its strengths and weakness.
2. Study your child(ren)'s personality.
3. Look at their strengths to see the possibilities of who they could become.
4. Write down ways you could better respond to each child according to his/her needs and personalities.

CHAPTER 4

Do You Love Me?

 PARENTING POINT: "There is nothing you can do to make me love you more and there is nothing you can do to make me love you less." Mark Gregston[9]

"Have you seen my phone?"

"No. When did you last have it?"

Panic ensues. No phone means no connection. My son offers a reward to his siblings for anyone who can find his phone. The car is scoured; pants pockets are searched; couch cushions are rifled through. Despair sets in; the phone has been missing since the day before. The search closes in on the bedroom where he took a nap. My son calls the phone again, hoping it still rings and the battery is not dead yet.

The faint ringing is heard. Everyone scrambles to uncover it first to get the reward. The teen who lost the phone triumphantly holds it up after finding it under a pillow. My youngest casually says, "Oh, I heard it ringing last night when I was trying to go to sleep!" (My teen is in disbelief that this critical piece of knowledge hadn't been shared as he has been tearing the house apart trying to find his phone.)

This isn't the first time a phone was lost and it won't be the last. However, every time it happens, the person who lost the phone feels tremendous anxiety. For many teens, that phone represents the most important connection they have to the world: the internet and their friends.

Technological changes have created a world that is very different from the one in which I grew up. The millennial generation is the first to have little-to-no knowledge of life without the internet. These kids are digitally connected to more people than ever—yet they often have a great sense of loneliness. Instead of growing up with only local influences, the whole world is at their fingertips. Yet in many cases, the past support systems—like a nuclear family, extended family, and the connection with neighbors—are no longer present for kids.

Teenagers and children need their parents now more than ever to navigate their way to adulthood. Fortunately, even in this digital age, I believe parents still have a lot of influence on their teens' thoughts and behaviors. This is why we need to both provide structure for our kids through rules (and consequences for breaking those rules) and ensure they feel loved and accepted. It is important to note the both-and of this statement; love and structured discipline cannot be without each other.

Discussing discipline can be difficult, but for many it's easier than discussing love, because it's the more tangible of the two. Fortunately, we have a tool to help us discuss how to better show love to our children: love languages. Just as we teach our children our spoken language so they can understand what we are saying, we must learn to speak in their love languages so they know and feel our love. Even if we love our children, if they don't *feel* our love, it will affect their motivation for learning, their ability to empathize with others, and even their emotional and spiritual growth. Oftentimes, children and teens act out when their love tanks are empty.

In this chapter, I will show how the love languages, created by Gary Chapman in his book, *The 5 Love Languages: The Secret to Love that Lasts*,[10] are expressed in my family and life, but I encourage you to visit the website www.5lovelanguages.com to help you learn your child's love language. Chapman also co-authored *The 5 Love Languages of Children: The Secret to Loving Children Effectively*[11] and *The 5 Love Languages of Teenagers: The Secret to Loving Teens Effectively*,[12] which I highly recommend as well. Understanding and applying love languages in the relationship with your spouse or significant other also makes a significant positive impact.

The five love languages are:

1. Touch
2. Words of Affirmation
3. Quality Time
4. Acts of Service
5. Receiving Gifts

Physical Touch

My youngest son greets me with a hug nearly every time he sees me! He takes any opportunity to snuggle in my lap, hold hands, and just hang out. Although he loves physical touch, he expresses love strongly with words and quality time, as well.

Touch is an important language for all children, especially in their early years. For babies, physical touch is not just natural—it is vital for their health. For infants, a lack of touch can cause failure to thrive as well as attachment and relationship problems later. It has been well-documented how children have struggled to grow and have often died when they have lacked touch as young children in orphanages.[13] Even in our current culture, it has always saddened me to see babies sitting in their car seats with bottles propped up for their feedings instead of being held. The wide availability of car seats, strollers, swings, bouncy chairs, and the like means that a baby can go from one to another. You don't even have to touch the child anymore—just click the seat into the next device. Do not underestimate the power of touch; hold your babies!

As my children have grown, I have had to be intentional to express my love through touch when they are too big to sit in my lap or too cool to hold hands. I have often taken advantage of them sitting next to me in church to rub their backs, or I can put my arm around their shoulder. Some of my kids love being tickled, and others don't. Be sensitive to what your children are expressing to you. My girls enjoy having me do their hair. Again, that feels amazing for some, but kids who have sensitive scalps do not find this pleasurable.

This may come naturally for you if you were raised in a touchy-feely home or have the love language of physical touch yourself. But if you're like me, this takes effort and is something that requires practice. Dave's primary love language is physical touch, and I can communicate well with him throughout the day, but it is more challenging for me to express this love language to my kids—especially as they have gotten older.

However, teens need physical touch just as much as they did when they were young, especially if this is their primary love language. You just need to make sure the timing (their mood) and place (not in front of peers) is appropriate to give them a hug or something like that. As a matter of fact, if the parent responds to that need for touch and fills their teens' love tanks, those teens may have less of a need to seek to fulfill this desire elsewhere, which can lead to healthier relationships with the opposite sex.

There are other ways you can communicate in this love language. For example, I got "The Stick," which is a tool for giving massages. I learned about it through my oldest son, who had been using one as part of his college swim team training. Since so many of my children are swimmers, I thought it would be great to get one, both to help ease sore muscles from practice and to provide another way to express the love language of physical touch. This worked out well, especially with my older boys who, like me, have physical touch as a less-important love language.

One mother I know did not grow up in an affectionate home, and so she found it difficult to express her love this way. However, after studying her daughter, she realized that touch was her daughter's primary love language. Over the course of one week, she intentionally took the time and effort to hug her daughter and sit with her. Even in such a short amount of time, the change in her daughter was drastic. She had tears in her eyes as she told me that for the first time, her daughter had chosen to go to her for a hug over her husband. She said her daughter was so much happier, and she could feel their bond growing stronger.

Words of Affirmation

Even at 5 years old, it is obvious that this is one of my youngest child's love languages. He often comes up to me saying, "I just love you," or "Did you like to see me swim today?" He also thrives on words of affirmation.

The saying, "Sticks and stones can break my bones, but words can never hurt me," is wrong. Words are extremely important and can either encourage or tear down a child. We are a mirror that reflects back to our children how we see and value them. How we respond and act, and the tone we use, are all part of this.

This does not mean that you should use flattery; instead, we must be sure to use words of true encouragement. For example, don't say, "You did an awesome job during the game!" when a child clearly had a bad day. Instead, say, "I see you had a rough game. Some days are like that. I'd love to practice with you this week; would you like that?" Children know the truth, so use genuine encouragement.

Josh, our oldest, has words of affirmation as his primary love language. He is a voracious reader. He has read more books than anyone I know, but I don't say, "You are so smart." Instead, I show an interest in what he is reading or passionate about. Similarly, as we have homeschooled our children, we don't talk about the grade level each kid reads at and compare them with the others; instead, we encourage each kid to pursue their interests.

Some kids will be good at reading, and some at math, or science, or art. Some are highly academic, but others will struggle in school. Some kids are very compassionate; some are very detail-oriented; some are good at building things. One of these strengths isn't better than another. All children need encouragement and words of affirmation and acceptance for who God created them to be. Using words of endearment and encouragement shows that you love your child for who they are.

I like the way Chapman and Campbell define encouragement in *The 5 Love Languages of Children: The Secret To Loving Children Effectively*: "To instill courage." How often have we seen in our own lives that receiving encouragement results in us working harder and doing more? Likewise, we want to encourage our children to attempt more, and we can do so with our words. These words stay with a child.

Here are some examples of helpful encouragement I have used with my kids:

> "I love the heart you have for children with special needs. Alex's face lights up when he sees you."

> "I enjoyed baking cookies with you today."

> "When Asher got hurt today, I really appreciate the care and compassion you showed him."

> "I really like the colors you chose on that logo design. I can't wait to see what you do next."

Brainstorm other ideas about how you could encourage your children and write them down. Then make sure to sprinkle them throughout your day.

As we think about words of encouragement, we must also address words of criticism. Critical words and arguments are very harmful for any child, but they are even more damaging to a child whose love language is words of affirmation. How we speak, the volume of our words, or the tone we use can be either helpful or harmful. For example, if I want one of my children to go out and fill our bin with firewood, I could make the request a couple of different ways:

"Go get firewood, now!"

"Would you please bring in some firewood for me? I get so cold without the fire burning."

Both examples achieve my goal of asking for firewood to be brought in the house, but they will cause very different feelings in my child.

This is especially true for teenagers. Your teen will feel and respond differently depending on how you communicate. It may have been easy to say, "I love you," and "I am so proud of you," to a young kid, but with a teen who is challenging boundaries and being argumentative, these words can often be forgotten and replaced with condemnation.

Recognizing and encouraging *effort* is most important! There is nothing more deflating than working hard on something and then being criticized for not doing it well enough. This is *so hard* as a parent, and it is something I have to be careful not to do. When I ask my son to clean a bathroom and it is not done well, it is so easy to be critical. The message he gets is "Why bother? I did all that work and it is not appreciated." He will be less motivated to clean the bathroom. Encouraging his effort by thanking him for cleaning the bathroom will help him feel appreciated. After cleaning the bathroom for several weeks, he would be more open to some additional training if I say something like, "Thank you so much for cleaning the bathroom. It would be great if you could make sure the sink gets scrubbed clean as well. I find that the blue scrubby sponge works great to get the toothpaste off." So be sure to recognize and verbalize their efforts in doing the right thing and back off in criticism of what they didn't do right.

Specificity is also important. How many times do our children show us their drawing, the Lego creation they made, or other things they did or tried? It is important to take the time to say something specific—not simply, "That is nice." Share with your child what you *liked* about it, such as:

> "I love the color combinations your chose."

> "I really like how you built those wings on that plane."

> "I'm proud of you for trying this new recipe—the flavors are great!"

These words of affirmation are so important for all children and teens, but especially for those with this love language.

Quality Time

Quality time is giving someone your focused, undivided attention. In essence, you are giving them a portion of your life, free from other distractions. If you have a child who is constantly asking you to play a game, read a book, or go for a walk, or color together, her love language is probably quality time. When you say you are too busy or keep putting them off, it makes them feel unloved and unimportant. Even when I have things to do, I find it better to say, "Sure! Let's play for 15 minutes, and then I will need to get my work done." Spending intentional time with them, even in short stretches, will show them that you value them.

This love language takes more time and effort than words of affirmation or physical touch. Quality time is more than watching TV together or being in the same room in silence. Quality time involves engaging with your child, maintaining eye contact, actively listening—not interrupting or doing all the talking, but actively listening—to what your child is saying. In other words, multitasking is not giving quality time!

I have found that my teenagers often show up in our office late at night just to chat. Usually it happens when Dave and I have some wind-down time, or I need to get things done. But I still try to make sure I spend this time with my kids, because I know that it is so much more important to take advantage of that time when they are ready to talk.

Ask your kids what their favorite thing is to do as a family. You may be surprised at their answers. Often, they relish things that you can plan to do more regularly. For example, some of our kids say making s'mores by our fire pit in the backyard is at the top of their list of activities they enjoy, so we try to do this regularly as weather permits. Not only is making and eating them fun, but we can sit around the fire talking and enjoying each other's company. I also know all my kids *love* it when we play games with them. Some of our favorite family games are cards, dominoes, Guesstures, Bandu, or other group games like those. Visit parentingsensibly.com for more family game recommendations.

With our busy schedules, it can be easy to put off spending quality time together, but it is so important to intentionally carve out time for this connecting. I know this from experience, because this is my main love language. Quality time isn't about spending a lot of money on huge adventures, but about having focused, attentive time together. For example, my favorite thing is to spend time with Dave in our hot tub, which we purchased used for $200. I would much rather do that than go out to eat or go anywhere, because it seems to be the only time we can talk uninterrupted. It isn't a grand or expensive gesture, but having that time in the hot tub or taking the time to play a card game with my children makes a tremendous difference in the strength of our relationships.

Acts of Service

I always have to laugh when I talk about the love language of acts of service—after all, isn't that what most of us spend our life doing while raising children? Yet this is an important love language for many people.

Our everyday routines—cooking, cleaning, doing laundry, fixing broken things around the house, helping our children with various tasks throughout the day, and so on—are acts of service. Are we doing them with the right attitude, in a loving way?

When we serve our families, it should be done with a good attitude. If a child asks you to help with school work, and you huff and groan and complain, it is telling your child that he is a burden and that you don't really care about him. But by joyfully, willingly, lovingly helping your kids, it shows them you care about them.

Teaching, guiding, and training our children is an act of service. Many following chapters of this book will go into this in much more detail, but parenting isn't about doing everything *for* our kids; instead it is about teaching and guiding our children so they will learn to do things themselves. Come alongside your child to encourage and assist when needed, but don't do for them what they can do on their own.

Be there for your children when they get hurt, sick, or need help with a project or homework. When it comes to school projects, remember: Don't do it for them. But be there to offer help when they request it. Even if you aren't exactly sure *how* to help, the important thing is to encourage them in their effort. I remember getting sick at school one time, and my dad sent one of his employees to pick me up from school and take me home. I did not feel loved or cared for that day. But I remember other times when I was younger and my mom bought me sticker books to entertain me when I was home sick. That did make me feel loved and cared for. In either instance, my parents weren't able to fix the problem at hand—my illnesses—but having that personal touch made a tremendous difference in feeling loved.

Avoid using any kind of reasoning that says or suggests, "If you love me, you will...". Neither the child nor the parent should ever use this phrase that suggests love is conditional, having to be earned or proved. Instead love needs to be expressed as unconditional: "There is nothing you can do to make me love you more, and there is nothing you can do that will make me love you less."[14]

Remember to do what is best for your children—not just what would make them happy in that particular moment. For example, letting them eat whatever they want would make them happy in the moment but would not be in their best interest. This is hard, and I know it seems easier to just give in. However, these little decisions add up to be significant. Be intentional for your children's long-term good.

Finally, a huge part of acts of service is to model and provide regular opportunities for your children to serve others. This will bless your children by allowing them to bless others and take their eyes off themselves. It will also give children whose love language is acts of service opportunities to express that language to others, but it is important for all, regardless of their love language. (Read more on how serving others can help your family in Chapter 12.)

Receiving Gifts

While it's true that all children enjoy receiving gifts, those who have this as a top love language feel a much higher sense of love when they receive a gift, especially a thoughtful one. My mom's love language is gifts. I sent her a gift card for her favorite store one Christmas. She commented about the cute box the gift card arrived in and how she went to the store and picked out just the right thing. It is hard for my mom to send money—she gets much more joy and satisfaction in picking out, wrapping, and sending a thoughtful gift—but when she does, she carefully picks out a fun, musical card to send the money in. This is very common for those who have the love language of gifts; they often comment on the wrapping paper or the bow, and after it's opened, they talk about it, thank you profusely for it, and remember each gift, who got it for them, and why.

For those with this love language, the gifts they give and receive don't have to be expensive or extravagant to make them feel loved. For example, Sophia's top love language is gifts. When she gets a gift, she lights up and runs over to hug me. She is also constantly making gifts to give to her friends and family. I often find a picture, a little felt sewing craft, or a note on my bed stand that Sophia has placed there some time during the day. She made personalized pictures to hang on each bedroom door. These are simple ways she enjoys getting gifts and giving them to others. Gifts is also the love language of my youngest daughter, Katie. She carefully budgets her money to make sure she can get something for each person in our family for birthdays or Christmas. She will find something that person will enjoy in the one-to-two-dollar range.

In our current culture, there are many things that we think of as everyday purchases for our loved ones—including our children—that are actually gifts that we can (and should) learn to appreciate. Gifts of necessity are both highly valued and appreciated; what's considered a necessity can be up for debate, though. When Dave's Grandma Josie was asked, near the end of her life, what her most memorable Christmas gift was, she recalled a manicure set she received when she was 7 years old. Her father had died while working in the mines in Idaho, leaving her mother a widow with five young children. Since there was no life insurance or other benefits, her mother moved the family back to South Dakota and worked whatever jobs she could—washing clothes, ironing, mending, and other odd jobs—to provide for the family. Having so little meant that every gift—even a simple manicure set—meant a great deal to Grandma Josie. I think today's kids don't often appreciate the food, clothes, and other things they receive, so we try to instill that gratitude and awareness in our children.

As with acts of service, the *why* behind a gift is important to remember. The Greek word for gift is *charis*, meaning "grace or an undeserved gift." A true gift is an expression of love, not a payment for something. It loses its association with love if it is given as a bribe or as a substitution for love. It is not uncommon for gifts to children to be given because of a parent's guilt—perhaps from working long hours, perhaps because of a divorce that has separated a family, or any number of other reasons. A gift given out of guilt or as a bribe will not have the same positive effect; instead, it can easily cause anger and resentment, particularly when children are older and more aware of what is going on around them. For example, if a parent promises to spend an evening with a child, but the parent cancels last minute and sends them a gift instead, the gift loses its specialness.

Again, the cost of the gift is not what matters for those who have this as their love language; intention and love do. A gift might be a sticker on a paper well done. It could be making a child a scrapbook or other photobook filled with fond memories. Gifts cannot be given alone without expressing your love in all the other ways as well. The child will need the presence of words of affirmation, loving touch, acts of service, and quality time for love to be felt through the gifts. For example, if a parent is distant and only sends gifts, but has no other contact with a child, the child will not feel a loving relationship, no matter if the parent's gifts are sent in kindness and love.

One final thought to remember regarding gifts: Your children should be given regular opportunities to *give* so that their focus is not always on themselves. Especially if it does not come naturally for your child, be on the lookout for ways to encourage them to provide gifts for others, inside or outside your family.

This week, start your investigation to learn the love languages for both your significant other and your children so that you can speak love in their languages. Completing online surveys will probably be harder for younger children, especially those who are still learning to express themselves, so observation may be the best way to figure this out. Experiment to see how your child responds to the different love languages. Give them a hug or a back rub; play a game together or bake cookies together; give them an encouraging word; willingly help them with homework or another task; and give them a small but thoughtful gift. Over time, it will become more obvious which love language is their primary one. Love languages can change over time, however, and it is important to speak in all forms of love languages; just pay special attention to what seems to speak loudest for each individual child.

I have also found it helpful to have my older kids do a survey to identify their love languages. Once you have this information, work on using that knowledge and being intentional on showing that child love in their own language.

For more information, please read *The 5 Love Languages* books. They are very helpful and go into greater depth on this topic.

1. Go to: http://www.5lovelanguages.com/ and click "Learn your Love Language" to take the love language profiles.

2. What is your love language?
   Your significant other's love language?

3. Child's Name_____ Love Language_____
   Child's Name_____ Love Language_____
   Child's Name_____ Love Language_____
   Child's Name_____ Love Language_____
   Child's Name_____ Love Language_____

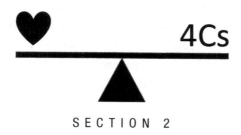

4Cs

SECTION 2

Foundations of Discipline

Exercise. Some people love it, others despise it, but most people agree that some level of exercise is important to keep your body healthy. For me, exercise was something I avoided. Whenever I exercised, I was riddled with feelings of inadequacy that stemmed from bad experiences as a child: always the last one picked to be on a team; always finishing in the rear of any swim team race; always wrestling with the feeling that I just was not athletic. I wrote off exercise and instead watched what I ate. However, as I aged, it became very obvious that no matter how much I changed my food intake, exercise was necessary to maintain my health. I didn't want people to see how out of shape and uncoordinated I was, so I did the one thing I could do: I walked.

We bought a very cheap, used treadmill, which allowed me to slowly increase my speed and the difficulty of my workout hidden away from all eyes—no one would see me walking in my furnace room! As I huffed and puffed, I realized how out of shape I had let myself become, and I was determined to keep working on improving my fitness.

After 8 months of consistent effort, I had built up enough confidence to try one more thing: yoga. Again, in the seclusion of my own home, I tried some free yoga videos I found online and settled on a few I liked. Alternating between fast treadmill walking and yoga gave me the confidence to try another free online exercise routine, this time adding light hand weights and cardio routines. At this point I had been exercising for a year, but even doing one minute of jumping jacks was too much—between having 10 kids and not having much core strength, every jump made me wonder if my internal organs would fall out! But I was determined to keep getting healthier, so I didn't quit—I just modified the exercises to be able to work around my body's limitations.

Over time, my body strengthened, and I was able to do longer and harder workouts. After two years of increasing the difficulty of my workouts, I am amazed at the results I've gained because of my newfound discipline and commitment to stick with it. Even though I have known all my life that it would be good for my health if I worked out, I came up with every excuse to avoid it: I'm too busy; I don't know how; I'm not athletic. It wasn't until I was weary of fighting the body changes that come with aging that I finally stepped out of my comfort zone and started exercising. Once I made that decision and made exercising a priority in my day, I could finally reap the benefits of a healthier body.

If I, as an adult, struggle at times with self-control and doing the right thing, think about how much more children will struggle with it. It will take time, experience, and lots of patience to help our children mature into adulthood. No method of discipline will work 100 percent of the time, but through consistent, balanced love and discipline, you will see your child start to learn, grow, and establish self-control.

How we respond in moments of frustration or even anger at a child's disobedience can either help or hinder this process. It takes planning and forethought to learn to respond effectively, rather than react. Many of you may find yourself questioning what you have done so far in your parenting journey. Though it is important to reflect and understand how you have arrived at this point, it is even more important to let go of the past and focus on how you can best move forward. It won't be easy to move forward; like my exercise journey, it will require small changes, modifications, and not a little bit of sweat. But over time, those small changes lead to tremendous difference.

The following chapters are filled with core discipline principles that have helped me tremendously over the years. I want to acknowledge Betty Chase's *Discipline Them, Love Them* workbook[15] and Barb

Tompkins' Moms Class[16] that I attended at The Journey Church in Tucson, Arizona. The principles taught using that workbook and Barb's teaching laid this foundational knowledge. Chapters 5-8 contain some common content in a similar format to that which Betty Chase used, along with my experiences and how the application of these principles has worked well for me. This book is a compilation of the things I have found most instrumental in my parenting journey.

It will be most beneficial if you read chapters 5-10 in sequential order to fully understand the big picture, since the concepts build upon each other. These principles have helped me and many others to develop strategies that allow the practice of disciplining my children to be carried out in a consistent manner and with love, not anger. Read each chapter, take the time to consider ways that you can apply these ideas, and bring them to life in your home.

4Cs

CHAPTER 5

Discipline versus Punishment: How to Tell the Difference (and Why It Matters)

 PARENTING POINT: We can't control our children, but we can train them. (Barb Tompkins[17])

When Dave was on his high school's basketball team in rural Iowa, his coach would run a drill where everyone would line up and attempt to shoot a free-throw. If the shot was missed, the whole team would have to run three sprints, and then get back in line. The penalty for missing did nothing to train them to become better at free-throws, but they became great runners!

The same can be true in our homes. If one child hits another while they are fighting over a toy and we punish by spanking, we are reinforcing the opposite of the lesson we want to teach. If we want to teach our children how to resolve an argument or what they can do when they get frustrated and angry, a better option would be to offer a cool-down time first, then come together to help the kids negotiate a solution. It is better to teach and train through discipline than to punish.

So, What is the Difference Between Punishment and Discipline?

Often, the words discipline and punishment are used interchangeably, and both seem to have a negative connotation. When "discipline" is defined, "punishment" is used as or as part of the definition. But when I looked in the dictionary, the entry for "discipline" noted an obsolete meaning: instruction.[18] It is easy to lose the "instruction" aspect of discipline.

According to Merriam-Webster, punishment means "suffering, pain, or loss that serves as retribution," or "a penalty inflicted on an offender through judicial procedure," or "severe, rough, or disastrous treatment."[19] When looking at the definition of punishment, we see it is not the way we want to parent our children. Yet it is confusing when we talk about the need to discipline our children and the first definition of discipline is punishment.

I want you to fully understand what I mean, though, when I refer to discipline. First, let's look at its root word and word origin. The root word of discipline is "disciple," which means "learner." The Latin word *disciplina* means "instruction given, teaching, learning, and knowledge."

When someone asks a college student what academic discipline she's studying, the question clearly has nothing to do with punishment. It is about a field of study or a branch of knowledge. But our common usage of the word has changed "discipline" to only mean "correction," and thus has lost the instruction part!

Throughout this book, when I refer to "discipline," I am referring to teaching, guiding, and training. Someday our children will grow up and leave home, and I strongly believe that our role as parents is to help prepare them for adulthood—that is, to discipline them.

This chart explains the difference between punishment and discipline.

PUNISHMENT	DISCIPLINE
Penalty for past wrongs	Train for better choices in the future
Anger	Love
Feeling: Fear, shame, and resentment	Feeling: Security
Result: Temporary obedience or rebellion	Result: Growth and maturity

We Discipline our Children Because We Love Them.

Today, it's common for many parents to want to be their child's friend. To show love, they give their child everything the child wants and avoid doing or saying anything that makes the child unhappy. The outcome of this style of parenting, however, is less than desirable: Often, the child can become self-centered, unappreciative, and lacking in respect. I believe that these parents truly love their children, but they are missing a key element in their parenting that children need: discipline. Children are looking to us for guidance on how to navigate through the ups and downs of life and prepare them for their future independence. The attitude should be: **I discipline my children <u>because</u> I love them.**

On the other end of the spectrum, there are parents who focus primarily on obedience through punishment. On the surface, these children submit out of fear, but the relationship between the parent and child suffers. The focus needs to shift to discipline and training, not punishing, and be more balanced by love.

So how do we train/discipline?

The 4 Cs

1. **COMMUNICATE** - Use clear communication to discuss expectations. (See Chapter 7 on communicating effectively.)
2. **COACH** - We should view ourselves as our children's life coach, encouraging, teaching, and guiding them, so when they leave our homes at 18, they will have the skills needed to navigate life independently. In this step, provide teaching and training on whatever you expect your child to do.
3. **CONSEQUENCE** - There are consequences for any choice we make, positive or negative. (See Chapter 8 for more on natural and logical consequences.)
4. **CONNECTION** - Apologies and forgiveness provide an opportunity for reconciliation and to restore our connection with our child.

COMMUNICATE first. *Never discipline your child for something you haven't already taught them.* Before the Mom's Class, this was something I had never thought about. It forced me to think about the many situations in which I had reacted to something my children did that was wrong, and it made me realize how many of those situations occurred even though I had never previously shown my children what was *right*.

Can you think about a time when you made an error and did something that you truly didn't know was wrong and someone reacted strongly? It makes you feel terrible; if you had just known about it, you could have avoided the situation altogether. How can we expect our children to just "know" how and what to do? They are looking to us to train and guide them. Yes, this step takes time, but it will pay off immensely in the long run. It gives the child the ability to know what our expectations are and how to do what we expect.

For example, one common problem is getting your child to clean up his toys. Using the 4 Cs, the first step would be to *communicate* what you expect; you want him to clean up his toys each day before dinner. You will use this time to explain that you will *coach* him *how* to clean up the toys. You will also discuss the *consequence*, what will happen if the child does not pick up his or her toys. The consequence may be that the toys that were not picked up will be put away for a day or a week, depending on the age of the child and the situation.

COACHING is the second step. Coaching provides an opportunity to work with your child: In the cleaning up example, perhaps this happens by showing him where the toys go and what level of picking-up is expected. You will need to have toy bins, baskets, or another place to put the toys to make it manageable and age appropriate for the child. Just as adults need practice and training, so do children. Depending on the age of the child, you may have to stay in the coaching mode for several days until they learn how to do it. This works even with a young child; just make it a fun game. After you have done the instructing, give your child an opportunity to test the waters. When it is time for the child to pick up the toys from that day's play, you can reaffirm what you had taught him yesterday:

"Remember how we picked up the toys yesterday? Today it is your turn to pick up the toys. I am going to set the timer for 15 minutes; let's see how fast you can put them away. When you are done it will be dinner time. Remember, the toys you don't pick up will be put up high so you won't get to play with them tomorrow. However, I know you can put them away, and it is so awesome to see you grow up and take responsibility for your things."

CONSEQUENCE is the third step. A child needs a consequence when he or she knows your expectations but doesn't follow them. The goal is to alter or adjust the child's behavior by taking action, which encourages him to follow the prior instructions the next time. There are different methods of consequences that we will examine in the next chapters.

Expect your child to test the boundaries! He will see if you really mean what you say, especially if you haven't consistently followed through in the past. Here is where the testing comes into play. Some children enjoy this new picking-up-after-themselves expectation; others will have no interest and may even sulk and refuse to pick up the toys. When the timer goes off, just go around, place the toys into a box, and put them up high on a shelf. There is no need to scold or get angry; just let the consequence do the teaching. At first, the child may not care if the toys are put away, but over time, as the number of toys they can play with shrinks, they will start to get more motivated to pick them up.

The important final step is **CONNECTION**. This is where reconciliation occurs and your relationship is restored. I have found that there are times when the consequence occurs, but the child was fully aware it would happen and they just accept it. Other times, the child is very upset. It is very important to have this final step of connection when the child calms down. You can discuss the situation, what was supposed to happen, and what the child did to receive the consequence. Just like you coached him through how to pick up his toys, it is important to coach him through this reconciliation process. Kids don't automatically know how this works until you do so. Explain that you love him and want him to grow up to be responsible for his things. It is helpful to ask him questions, get him to explain what he was supposed to do and what he chose to do. It is important that the child acknowledges his poor choice. Even though you need to stand firm in the consequence, encourage him that tomorrow he will get another opportunity to pick up his toys. Go through apologies if needed, give him a nice hug, and tell him how much you love him.

The concept of the 4 Cs is applicable for all ages. As our children become teens and grow and mature, responsibility and accountability change. We need to loosen the reins and allow our children to take some test flights so that when they leave, they are prepared.

For example, each state has a certain amount of mandatory training an individual has to complete to get a driver's license. There is classroom learning and actual driving practice time. Anyone who has been through teaching a child to drive knows the stress of sitting in the passenger seat, white knuckles clinched on the door handle, wishing there were a brake pedal at your feet! I would prefer to have Dave put in the first 20 hours of practice, but because I am home more, I end up doing the majority of the practice driving time. At first, it seems the teen will never get the hang of it; corners are cut too sharp, too wide, or too fast, and the accelerations are too fast or too slow.

Over time, the teen starts to get the feel of the road, the car, and how to maneuver through various situations. By the time each teen finishes all their required practice hours, I start to feel better about their driving ability. All through this process, they have been taught and coached and have learned through consequences, right? When they turned too fast and felt the car tilt a bit and hearts were racing, they learned to slow down when turning. When they turned a corner and went up over the curb with the back tire, they learned to take a wider turn. It seems so logical in this setting, but this is just how we should view parenting in *all* areas.

Once a teen has her license and can legally drive alone, she has to be given the opportunity to venture out and test things. Some boundaries are set up by the state during the probationary period regarding who can be in the car with teens, hours a teen can drive, and so forth.

Parents can also set up some boundaries and consequences. Discuss any consequences ahead of time. For example, you may have the rule that if your child gets a ticket while driving, he will have to pay for that ticket and any increase in insurance premiums. At first, you may allow him to drive to the grocery store or to work. Over time, if he is being responsible, you can give him more freedoms, like being able to drive to a movie.

The 4 Cs framework can be applied to any age. This is just an introduction to this concept, and we will revisit it later in the book. As I stayed consistent with the 4 Cs, I saw a big improvement in our family. There were fewer battles, the kids obeyed more quickly, and I found myself getting angry less often.

Willful Defiance or Childish Irresponsibility

As we consider the 4 Cs model and the various methods of discipline available to us when a child disobeys, it is important to distinguish between two types of behavior that require discipline, as they will require different strategies:

- **WILLFUL DEFIANCE.** This is when a child knows what is expected but knowingly and defiantly does the opposite.
- **CHILDISH IRRESPONSIBILITY OR IMMATURITY.** This is when a child does not know or has not been taught what is the correct thing to do.[20]

It is so important to take a step back and look at the child's age, development, and whether or not you have trained him on a particular expectation.

For example, when a toddler is going through potty-training and is learning to wipe himself, he may use too much toilet paper, which can result in a clogged, overflowing toilet. This situation didn't occur because of willful defiance; it happened because he used too much toilet paper trying to clean himself and didn't understand how that could cause a huge mess. Did you take the time to go through training on how to wipe? Did you have the child practice several times with your supervision and instruction? Did you remember to discuss what would happen if too much toilet paper was used? Do not discipline a child who is just doing a developmentally normal behavior.

On the other hand, a friend once told me of how her two sons, who were 7 and 9, purposely jammed lots of toilet paper into the toilet and kept flushing over and over, laughing as water flooded the bathroom. It leaked through the floor and caused serious damage. This behavior was intentional and needed to have a consequence implemented.

It is normal behavior for a 12-month-old to grab at something of interest. They also drop things to the floor, which we call the "gravity game." The child drops food or a cup to the floor from a high chair and you pick it up. At first you think the child just dropped it, but after several times, you see the child is entertained, watching you pick up the item over and over. This is a normal developmental behavior at this age. Instead of disciplining in this situation, just stop picking up the dropped item and the game is over. Now, if an 8-year-old is playing the gravity game with fragile items in your house over the stairway railing, that requires a consequence.

Another example of a normal developmental behavior is a crying baby. Crying is a baby's way of communicating. They aren't trying to be mean or make you angry. Something is wrong, and they have no other way of communicating. So please, do not yell at a baby to be quiet. This will not have any positive result in the situation. Please take some time to learn about child development and the stage your child is currently in, as this will be very helpful. The American Academy of Pediatrics' website, www.healthychildren.org, is an excellent resource.[21] You will start to know the difference between normal developmental behavior and willful defiance that requires consequences. However, when the behavior is just childish irresponsibility or an accident, there can be teaching and training without the need for consequences.

Check Your Attitude – It's Contagious

When we think about how to discipline our children, it's important to get our reason right. Remember: We are training and disciplining—not punishing—our children *because* we love them. The parent's attitude is key. Depending on your attitude, the same consequence can come across as either punishment or discipline:

> **SCENARIO 1:** Two brothers are arguing. A parent walks into the room and yells, "Go to your rooms right now, and don't come out until I say so!"

> **SCENARIO 2:** Two brothers are arguing. A parent walks into the room and calmly says, "I see you two are upset. Please go to your rooms so you can have some time to cool down. After a few minutes, we will sit down together to talk to each of you about why you were angry and come up with a solution or compromise."

Both situations have the same consequence of going to their rooms, but one is done in anger with no element of training and resolution. Remember that we are training our children so that one day they will have the skills and character traits needed to thrive when they are adults, fathers, mothers, and spouses.

Also, be aware that attitudes—good or bad—are contagious. I love the children's book *The Quarreling Book*[22] by Charlotte Zolotow. It begins with the husband forgetting to kiss his wife good-bye on a rainy morning, which leads the mother to make a harsh statement to her son. As the day progresses, each person is rude and short tempered with the next person they meet. Isn't this so true of our everyday lives? I have seen this in my own home—more than once. When someone wakes up grumpy, it spreads through the whole house like a wildfire until everyone is grumbling.

The turning point in the story comes when the boy returns from school and pushes his dog off his bed. The dog doesn't realize it was done in anger; he thinks the boy is playing. The dog's playful response turns the boy's mood around, so he in turn is kind to his sister. That kindness then spreads down the line all the way back to the mother, just as the sun comes out and her husband returns from work.

I love this book because it speaks so clearly to me about how our attitude, good or bad, can affect others. As parents, we can consciously choose happiness and stop the negative attitude chain in our homes. We can't always choose circumstances, but we can choose how we respond to them. In Barb's parenting class, she always said, "Happiness is a choice!"[23] It truly is. We can choose happiness and so can our kids. It won't be easy, but it will make a big difference for everyone.

Attitudes

The longer I live, the more I realize the importance
of choosing the right attitude in life.
Attitude is more important than facts.
It is more important than your past;
more important than your education or financial situation;
more important than your circumstances, your successes, or your failures;
more important than what other people think, say, or do.
It is more important than your appearance, your giftedness, or your skills.
It will make or break a company. It will cause a church to soar or sink.
It will make the difference between a happy home or a miserable home.
You have a choice each day regarding the attitude you will embrace.

Life is like a violin.
You can focus on the broken strings that dangle,
or you can play your life's melody on the one that remains.
You cannot change the years that have passed,
nor can you change the daily tick of the clock.
You cannot change the pace of your march toward your death.
You cannot change the decisions or the reactions of other people.
And you certainly cannot change the inevitable.

Those are the strings that dangle!
What you can do is play on the one string that remains—your attitude.
I am convinced that life is 10 percent what happens to me
and 90 percent how I react to it.
The same is true for you.

Charles R. Swindoll[24]

With this in mind, we can make sure that we have the right attitude, even when our children give us a bad attitude. When your child is misbehaving, stop, talk, and listen. Set up a conversation with them: "I can see you are frustrated. Let's talk about it." Step back and think about why this child is acting this way. He may have had a hard day at school; perhaps she had a fight with a sibling. It may even be that he is simply tired.

One time, Nate was eating some animal crackers, and Katie, who was about 2 years old, wanted some. So Nate gave her one from his hand and then handed her the container of crackers. But Katie didn't want *those* animal crackers. She wanted the ones in Nate's hand—*all* of them. She threw herself on the floor and started screaming and thrashing. This went on and on, and she just could not pull herself together. This was very out of character for her, and it was obvious that she was too tired. I knew that disciplining at any level would be pointless. So instead I carried the sweaty, upset bundle upstairs, snuggled with her, and read some books; she promptly fell asleep.

Amusingly, for the next several weeks, Katie told several casual acquaintances about her fit and how Mom took her up to bed "'cause I was just too tired." Even at her young age, Katie knew she was making poor choices and wasn't rational, but she was too tired and out of control to reel it back in. Don't we all feel that way sometimes?

Now, I am not saying you should make excuses for bad behavior. However, there are times when we have to use discernment to determine whether discipline is truly needed, or if there are other factors at play that need to be considered.

Anger

Children are keen at detecting anger in their parents. Anger can lead to yelling, hitting, hurtful words, and regretful situations. I know what it is like to be a child with an angry father. When we would get too giggly around the dinner table or in the car, my dad's blood pressure would rise; you could *feel* the anger. We would try to avoid the arm swinging back in the station wagon, which was meant to quiet us down, *now*! One time, I had done something wrong (for reasons I can no longer remember), and I knew I was going to get a spanking. I ran to my bedroom and locked the door. When I heard the bobby pin in the lock and the door opening, I was terrified. My dad looked at me crouched in the corner, scared to death; I think he felt badly at that moment, so he left the room without giving me a spanking.

I never wanted my kids to be fearful of me or to wonder day-to-day what mood I was in. To be punished by my father for a minor infringement because of other stressors or the influence of alcohol made me angry, hurt, and resentful. It put a wedge in our relationship. If you sense fear in your children, this is a red flag signaling an area you need to work on.

Sometimes when I was a kid and my parents determined I was "talking back," I was sharply reprimanded. But what constituted "talking back" puzzled me. I felt as though I was not allowed to discuss or give a different viewpoint. My father has shared more about his upbringing is recent years: He, like many people, was raised with this strict authoritarian way of "my way or the highway," which impacted his own parenting style. By the grace of God, he is an amazing man today (as I will share in Chapter 17). For me, however, being reprimanded for simply speaking was very degrading, and it tore apart our relationship for many, many years.

Anger exists. It is an emotion we all feel. But what we *do* with that anger can either cause us to react in a harmful way or respond appropriately to address the situation productively. It is important to start thinking about the triggers. What causes us to feel angry? Is it when our children don't respond to our regularly repeated request? Is it the constant bickering? Is it hearing disrespectful attitudes? Is it due to lack of sleep? Is it a messy house? Is it financial or marital stress? Is it an over-packed schedule? Start jotting down what triggers anger for you.

Think about your goals as a parent. Yelling and losing control with our kids is not going to help us accomplish our goal of teaching self-control. How are they going to learn that if we are constantly losing control ourselves? If we don't want our children to think that yelling is part of a healthy relationship, we need to model healthy behavior instead.

You may be thinking, "Yeah, but I feel so much better after I yell and get my anger out." Kevin Leman gives a great analogy in *Have a New Kid by Friday*.[25] He says to picture an angry outburst like vomiting all over your child. Yes, you feel much better after you get it all out; however, the child doesn't. He is covered in nastiness, and those words cannot be taken back. We are there to love, train, and encourage our children, not crush them. There are two ways a child will respond to yelling in the home: They will become quiet and retreat into a shell, or they will become rebellious. Neither situation is one we want.

Respond, Don't React

In thinking about dealing with our anger, we really want to *respond*, not *react* to situations. This is going to take self-awareness and serious effort to stop, pause, and make an intentional decision on the best way to respond, instead of reacting to your first emotional impulse. This is the most difficult—but the most important—thing to do when you react out of anger. Anger is a signal. Each situation when it appears will be different, but you can develop a plan for when that signal comes—a plan that involves taking a moment to compose yourself and gather your thoughts as you think through how best to parent in that instant. That way, you will be prepared for that inevitable moment when you get angry, so that you can constructively respond instead of immediately react.

Here are some ways to cope if you do get angry:

1. Don't correct when angry—wait!

2. Walk to another room; leave the situation if you are feeling angry and go into your bedroom, bathroom, or some other place to regroup.

3. Do what it takes for you to calm down. Pray, meditate, listen to soothing music, take deep breaths, go for a short walk around the house—whatever it takes to help you regain control.

4. Discern *why* you are angry. What brought this situation to this place? Figuring out the triggers or coming up with a plan for how to address the situation or prevent it in the future is very helpful.

5. When you are calm and have decided how you are going to reasonably respond, you can implement your plan.[26]

One thing that is immensely helpful is working as a team with your spouse or significant other if you have one. It's very rare that my husband and I are both angry at the same time. When I sense that my husband's frustration is escalating, I gently step in to handle the situation and let him leave. He does the same for me. Neither one of us wants to get angry and lose control, so by working together, we can parent more effectively. This is never done with an angry, disgusting, belittling undertone, but in an "I got your back" way. I can say, "Honey, I have some thoughts and ideas I'd like to try. Why don't you take a break, and I'll see what I can do?" No one likes that feeling of losing control—or being called out on it—but if you can dialog ahead of time about how to work together to parent more effectively, it can be a huge relief to be able to leave and calm down. When this has happened, Dave and I usually talk privately about the situation afterward, what we could have done differently, and where we should go from here. Remember, you are on the same team!

One additional consideration: If you are feeling short with the kids, it might be about you instead of your kids. Try to evaluate where your problems are coming from. Are you tired or feeling depressed? Is your marriage or relationship with your significant other in a rocky place? Are you frustrated with your parenting situation? Have you been very permissive and now your kids are demanding and disrespectful? Are you having work stress, or is your schedule too packed?

If you are feeling stressed, take a step back and figure out where the stress is coming from. Work on getting that situation taken care of so you are not reacting to the kids and taking it out on them. My top stress relieving tip: Exercise. I know, I know what you're thinking: Anything but *that*! But as I mentioned earlier, a couple years ago I came to the realization that I *needed* to start exercising—not just for my physical needs, but for my mental needs as well. Even five minutes of aerobic exercise can have anti-anxiety effects! All of this will help us to *respond*, not *react*.

Here are things to keep in mind as you continue to learn to *respond* first:[27],[28]

1. Be a positive role-model. Things are *caught*, not *taught*: Children learn more by watching than by listening to what you say.

2. Balance discipline with love. Discipline without relationship leads to rebellion.

3. Apply the 4 Cs:
   a. *Communicate* first.
   b. Take the time to *coach*.
   c. Follow through with *consequences*. Don't give 10 warnings first, because then you are teaching them not to respond the first nine times.
   d. *Connection*. Apologize. We are going to mess up—we all do—but take the time to apologize to your kids when you react in anger, and teach them to apologize when they have wronged others. It also helps if there is a way to make restitution or amends for what they did wrong. Make sure to

tell your child that you love them and forgive them. This step is essential for restoring relationships.

This won't be an overnight change. We all get angry. It is a normal emotion to feel. Raising children is hard, and they are experts at bringing out the not-so-good things in us. However, we need to take the time to develop a strategy for when that anger wells up, so that we can learn to respond in a healthy manner. No one is perfect, and we are going to blow it sometimes. Apologize. Explain to your kids that you shouldn't have reacted the way you did, and say you are sorry: "Mommy messed up. I am so sorry for yelling at you when you two were fighting. It isn't okay for you two to fight, but I shouldn't have yelled at you. Let's talk about what the arguing was all about and work through a solution. I love you two very much and want you to learn how to resolve a disagreement without fighting. Will you forgive me?" Keep working toward responding in a controlled manner; forward progress, no matter how small it seems, is good progress.

1. Take some time to write down things that trigger your anger.
2. Brainstorm some things you can do to decrease those stressors.
3. Write down some frequently occurring parenting challenges. Come up with a plan to implement using the 4 Cs.

4Cs

CHAPTER 6

Addressing Behavior Without Degrading the Child

 PARENTING POINT: Rules without relationship lead to rebellion.

In May 2016, a boy was left on the side of the road in Japan as punishment for throwing stones at cars and people. A few minutes later, his father returned to that spot to retrieve him, but his son was nowhere to be seen. What followed was a frantic six-day search by hundreds of volunteers, until the boy was found in an abandoned hut at a military facility three miles from where he was left. His father showed deep remorse and apologized during a press conference.

"We have raised him with love all along," he said. "I really didn't think it would come to that. We went too far. I thought we were doing it for my son's own good."[29]

Fortunately, this story had a happy ending, but it isn't hard to see how easily it could have gone fatally wrong. Discipline must be carried out in a thoughtful and careful manner, not done impulsively in anger.

We need to discipline in such a way that our children will be more likely to make better choices next time. We do not punish our children in ways that could harm them physically or emotionally. How do we discipline in love to help without harming or degrading them? When a child is crying and angry, does that mean we have broken her spirit? This chapter will address these questions and more.

Addressing issues of discipline is difficult, and as we dive into it you may feel overwhelmed. You may even start thinking of all the areas you want to change well before we have finished the discussion, and it may feel like an insurmountable task. Remember, we didn't get where we are in our parenting overnight; it took many years. In the same way, change is not going to happen overnight. Just take baby steps, focusing on one area at a time.

How we respond impacts how our child both responds to our discipline and sees our care for them as their parents. Remember, we are training and guiding our children because we love them. There are rules put into place to help them learn, grow, and be safe, and there are consequences when they break those rules, but the consequences can be carried out in such a way that the child learns from them and still feels the parent's love. This is where we have to get a handle on our anger so we can respond calmly and not simply react.

We must take care not to view abuse as discipline. Chart 1 compares abuse and discipline, outlining some of the differences and outcomes between the two. Discipline done correctly will not harm your children; instead, it will guide them to make better choices. Abuse is harmful. Please seek professional help if you are concerned that abuse may be happening in your family.

Now, let's revisit the chart of the four parenting styles (see Chart 2). Below each category is a list of the characteristics that a child raised in each parenting style may grow up to have as an adult. Our goal is to be the authoritative parent, in the upper right corner of the chart, whose child feels loved and has boundaries.[30]

Remember—this chart is *not* an absolute; each style is on a continuum. Parenting has no guarantees. However, we do know, through

ABUSE	DISCIPLINE
Done in anger	Done calmly with love
Humiliating	Not humiliating
Degrading	Respectful
Physical or emotional scars	No physical or emotional harm, reasonable and expected consequence
Harms self-esteem	Builds self-esteem, confidence
Unfair	Fair and balanced

CHART 1

AUTHORITARIAN PARENT	DISCIPLINE HIGH	AUTHORITATIVE PARENT
• Anxious • Insecure • Perfectionist • Resentful		• Secure • Responsive • Well-Adjusted • Respectful
LOW	**LOVE**	**HIGH**
UNINVOLVED PARENT	LOW DISCIPLINE	PERMISSIVE PARENT
• Wounded • Vulnerable • Angry • Unrestrained		• Self-Centered • Disobedient • Immature • Rebellious • Disrespectful

CHART 2

research,[31] that there are things we can do to increase the probability that our children will grow up to be well-adjusted, respectful, secure adults.

Several years ago, a mom with two young girls spoke to me about how dreadful it was to take her daughters into a store. She had fallen into a pattern of buying her daughters a doll *every time* they went shopping. The girls didn't need or care about the dolls, but the mother didn't want the fits that would result if she did not buy a doll. She had essentially dug herself into a deep hole. This is an example of a *permissive* parent. She loved her children, but without any boundaries the children were exhibiting the signs of those raised in a permissive household: self-centeredness, rebellion, and disrespect.

Dave's parents were *authoritative*. They didn't have a lot of spoken rules, like curfews, but they *did* have expectations that they assumed would be met, and they tried to show their children their love as well. Dave grew up to become the secure, well-adjusted, respectful person shown in the upper right quadrant. However, in the same house, with the same parenting style, his sister struggled during adolescence. Their parents loved watching the kids' sporting events and praised their athletic accomplishments. Dave's sister—who was not athletic—sometimes felt embarrassed and sad, and wondered about her place in the family. We will discuss this sort of situation further at a later point.

One person I know grew up in a home where her parents believed it was best for the children to figure things out on their own. To some extent this is important, but in her case, the kids had *no* training or help. She didn't feel an emotional connection or her parents' love. They lived their lives, and the kids lived theirs. She was thankful for a few other adults in her life who helped her, but her siblings have struggled with anxiety, depression, and addiction. Her parents were *uninvolved*, and it left the kids feeling lost.

My dad was *authoritarian*, as were his father and grandfather. There were no discussions: he made the rules and decisions and expected obedience. I certainly have struggled with insecurity and have perfectionistic tendencies. As a child I was anxious and nervous at what mood my dad would be in, and I was a very resentful teenager. However, there has been much healing and changing over the years, as you can read about in Chapter 17—firsthand proof that there is hope, that change can happen, and that relationships can be restored.

Parenting is hard. It takes a lot of intentional parenting to make sure each child feels loved and accepted. We need to have boundaries and make sure each child feels unconditional love.

Helping, Not Hurting

When boundaries are made, broken, and reinforced through discipline, your child will not be happy. But a child's anger does not mean he has been harmed; often, it's a natural reaction to the discipline. After all, *we* don't like it when someone calls out mistakes we've made or tells us about a negative behavior we need to correct. We also feel frustrated when we feel the consequences of our choices.

When you are disciplining, you need to keep separate the child from the behavior being disciplined. It is the bad behavior we are trying to correct, not the child we are trying to harm. Thus, make sure not to insult or humiliate the child. We are *training* them. As I mentioned in the last chapter, if *we* are losing control, we need to stop, remove ourselves from the situation to calm down, and develop an appropriate plan.

Discipline and love *must* go together. Think about love and discipline as oars on a rowboat. If you only row with love or only row with discipline, you will go in circles and never get anywhere! Discipline done right *is* love.

It's also important to remember that rules without relationship lead to rebellion. The balance between love and discipline is so important! Children need to know that you love them unconditionally and have a clear understanding of expectations and consequences by applying the 4 Cs.

Do You Love Me?

When parenting—especially when disciplining—it is important to assess the child's "emotional love tank." When it is on empty, you will see negative behaviors; those are the times we most need to show love and fill their emotional love tank. People give and receive love in different ways. In order to successfully fill a child's emotional love tank, you will need to understand how each of your children best feels loved.

Please refer to my chapter on how children feel loved (Chapter 4) to learn how to do this.

Regardless of how your children best recognize your love for them, put down all electronic devices and give your child focused attention. Look at them, talk about whatever is on their mind, read a book together, play a game, or go outside together. As tempting as the phone, tablet, or computer is, do not look at emails, texts, Facebook or anything; just give your child five, 10, or 15 minutes of your undivided attention. It will go a LONG way in helping them feel loved.

Today, many parents fall into performance-based love. Praise and love abound when kids do well in school or sports, but there is rejection and disapproval if they don't. This sense of rejection may not always be intentional. Earlier, I mentioned how Dave's sister felt when she was younger because she was not athletic like her three siblings. She saw herself as less valuable—and visible—than her siblings, even though this was completely unintentional on the part of her parents. Love should not be (nor be perceived as) conditional.

In an article called, "What Parents Should Say as Their Kids Perform,"[32] Tim Elmore, founder and president of the organization Growing Leaders, explains how problematic it is when parents fall into the supervisor role at their children's sports. They spend too much time coaching their kids or telling their coaches how to coach their kids. It stresses the child and makes her feel like she can never fully please her parents.

Instead of acting as pseudo-supervisors of our children's sports, we should offer encouragement and allow our children the space to grow up, make mistakes, and learn on their own. In his article, Elmore gives great examples based on research about the best ways for a parent to encourage.

"Before the Competition Say:	After the Competition Say:
1. Have fun.	1. Did you have fun?
2. Play hard.	2. I'm proud of you.
3. I love you.	3. I love you."

Elmore also noted that when college athletes were asked what words from their parents made them feel the best, their response was a simple phrase: "I love to watch you play." This phrase states no opinion about *how* they did; it just emphasizes that their parents loved to watch *them*, regardless of how well or how poorly they played that day.

God loves us unconditionally, and our kids need to know that you love them no matter what. You love them on good days and bad days, when they are doing well and when they are struggling. You love each one for the unique person God created them to be.

Clear Understanding of Expectations

As we discussed in the last chapter, accidents or situations where the child was never taught something should just be handled by coaching; there is no need for consequences. However, when children display willful disobedience, that needs to be addressed differently. When asked to do or not to do something and his "*no*" rings loud and clear, then you must address the situation. We will be going over discipline in much more depth in future chapters, but I want to walk you through one example here.

Example of Implementing the 4 Cs

We will be going over other discipline options in the upcoming chapters, but this is just one example that illustrates the steps you can take when a consequence is needed.

STEP 1: *COMMUNICATE CLEARLY.* Words may be all you need to use for the child to change the behavior. For example, when Katie was 3, she would constantly interrupt while I was doing school with the older children. When she was disruptive, I reminded her, "Katie, when I am reading and doing school with the older kids, you can play in this room, but you must play quietly. If you are not quiet, you will have to leave the room and play somewhere else. If you don't obey, you will have to go in a time-out." If she said, "Okay, Mom," and obeyed, that was the end of it.

STEP 2: *COACH IF NECESSARY*. In this scenario, my request was basic; other situations require coaching and training.

STEP 3: *CONSEQUENCE*. Using the example above, if Katie chose not to listen to my words and continued to be loud and disruptive, I would remind her what we talked about: "Katie, remember I asked you to play quietly in the room while we are doing school. Since you continue to be loud, you will have to play in a different room. If you refuse to play in another room so that we can work in here, you will have to go in a time-out." If she played quietly in another room, that was the end. If she became defiant, refused to leave the room, and started screaming, she had to go in a time-out.

STEP 4: *CONNECTION*. When the child has calmed down and is able to talk and accept responsibility for his action, it is time to talk and have resolution and reconciliation. This is vital, as it both helps the child process the lesson they learned from this incident and models how to reconcile and apologize in a healthy way. The process involves four steps:

1. I'm sorry for…
2. This is wrong because…
3. In the future, I will…
4. Will you forgive me?

With young children, you will need to teach them what to say to apologize. Once you have gone through this process a few times, they will know what to do when they are older.

Using the example from above as an illustration, here is what it may look like.

> "Katie, do you know why you are in a time-out? What were you doing when we were trying to do school?"
>
> "I was being loud."

"Yes. When we are doing school in the family room, it is okay for you to play in there, but you must play quietly. Otherwise, you can't play in that room. What did you do when I asked you to go play in another room?"

"I started screaming."

"It is time for you to apologize and tell me why it was wrong. You say, 'I am sorry, Mom, for screaming.' Now, can you tell me why it was wrong to scream?"

"Because you couldn't do school."

"What will you do next time when we are doing school?"

"Play quietly."

"Yes. Now say, 'Will you forgive me?'"

"Will you forgive me?"

"Yes, Katie, I forgive you. I love you very much." I give a nice extended hug. Then I say, "Let's go back in the other room. You can play quietly where we are, or you can go play in your room. Which would you like to do?"

It is amazing the change in mood that takes place after the connection/reconciliation occurs. In this scenario, Katie no longer interrupted us, and she played quietly. It is so important to stay calm, have your child admit what they did wrong, and end with the restoration in your relationship. It also is healing for the parent once this reconciliation occurs.

I realize time-outs were popular when I started parenting 25 years ago and many people today disagree with them. Over the years, there have been times when it was a logical choice and was very effective. It was just one option I used during certain situations of willful disobedience. Just like I need to go into another room to calm down at times, my children also had moments when they needed to have time to calm down. I talked to one of my 19-year-old twins the other day, and he said he remembers just needing to get away and have time to think and calm down. We would check on him and ask if he was ready to come out, and he would say, "NO!" Instead, he would come out when *he* was ready. There are still times when our 11-year-old twins get frustrated and go to their rooms for a while. They do this on their own and come down when they are ready. They don't want to talk to me or anyone when they are upset, but they will talk things over when they are ready.

Guilt Versus Shame[33]

As we consider how to discipline without causing harm, it is important to understand the difference between guilt and shame. It is fine for a child to feel guilt, but shame is damaging.

GUILT is when one *feels badly about their behavior*. When our children misbehave, we explain that we are disappointed in that behavior and why, but we also need to show them how they can make amends. This guides our children and helps them develop empathy and compassion for others. In helping our children with guilt, we want the message to be clear: We still love them, and we believe they will learn and do better in the future.

SHAME, on the other hand, is when one *feels like he or she is a bad person*. Parental anger, the withdrawal of love, or punishments that are too harsh for the misbehavior can lead to shame. When a child feels shame, they are likely to act out or withdraw. Shame is associated with addiction, depression, violence, suicide, and eating disorders.

Kids need boundaries and guidance, *and* they need to know that we love them. If the child gets some sort of correction, with no apology or reconciliation alongside it, then they do not get that important step of restoration with you. Without the reconciliation, a child will not understand that you are disciplining because you love them. As Gary Smalley says in his book *The Key to Your Child's Heart,* "True restoration is confession of wrong plus forgiveness granted."[34]

This process takes time and is sometimes difficult for us. We may be repeating some unhealthy patterns or still be harboring resentment from our childhood. Believe that you can change how you respond and can teach your children healthier ways to work through conflict. Let's talk about the important points:

- We need to address issues as they happen, instead of letting things go on and on until we become unglued. Often, it is a lot of work to address a child's problematic behavior, and we may be busy doing something, or perhaps we don't feel like dealing with the situation. However, when we wait, often our anger escalates. If you are already angry, don't address the situation until you have calmed down and have carefully thought through your next steps.

- *Don't bring up the past* when disciplining for a present action. This consequence is for this situation, not for dredging up all the past hurts, habits, and hang-ups. Absolutes like "always" and "never" should be avoided. I once overheard a teen arguing with his parents; both sides were bringing up all kinds of past mistakes, and I knew it was a losing battle for both sides. It was clear that there hadn't been reconciliation or forgiveness; instead, a collection of hurts had grown like a snowball rolling downhill. With this pattern, the cycle of hurt and frustration keeps building. It is so important to deal with the issue at hand and go through the process of discipline *and* reconciliation.

- Don't use name-calling. Remember, we are addressing the behavior, not the child. We want them to make different choices, not belittle them! We are a mirror, and what we say is reflected back to them and affects how they see themselves.

- Respond, don't react. *We must not react to our own feelings.* Instead, we must respond to misbehavior with intentional, reasoned choices. If you are angry, you must walk away and calm down first. Anger totally clouds your ability to respond appropriately, so wait until you get control of yourself first.

We are Both Going to Mess Up

Jeff Kemp has a great example for us:

> "When my youngest son was 5 we were in the yard shooting baskets. Keegan was so small, the ball was so big, and the hoop was so high that he was lucky to even get the ball to hit the rim. But he was with his dad and having fun.
>
> I was watching him play, hoping that he'd make a basket, when he popped off with a line that I'll always remember: 'Daddy, I'm good at the shooting part. I'm just not good at the making part.'"[35]

As our children grow, we will see them make misses, rim shots, and baskets. Remember that this time is for teaching and training with love and grace. They may not always be "good at the making part," but we love them anyway as we are guiding them toward making better choices.

Remember: *Rules without relationship lead to rebellion.* Focus on the behavior, not the child. Make sure you have apologies and forgiveness, and don't forget that you can set the example by apologizing to your children and asking for their forgiveness when you mess up.

1. Is your child feeling shame or guilt when you discipline?
2. Does your child feel your unconditional love, or is it performance-based?
3. Are apologies and forgiveness modeled and practiced within your home, or are grudges for past misdeeds smoldering?

4Cs

CHAPTER 7

Say What? Communicating Effectively With Your Child

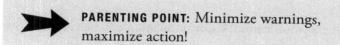

PARENTING POINT: Minimize warnings, maximize action!

Recently, a texting conversation between a mom and her 16-year-old daughter went viral. The mother found some pills in the daughter's nightstand while looking for a calculator; she sent a picture of the baggie and the text conversation was comical. The mother immediately assumed the pills were drugs and grounded her. Her daughter laughed and told her to put the pills in water. After doing so, the *pills* turned into sponge dinosaurs![36]

Both the mother and daughter (and everyone who shared the story online) found humor in the situation after the fact, but it highlights how important it is to communicate first before jumping to conclusions and handing out consequences.

In Chapter 5, we learned about the 4 Cs:

- **COMMUNICATE**: We must first outline to our kids what our expectations are.
- **COACH**: Next, we must train our children *how* and *why* we expect them to behave according to these expectations.
- **CONSEQUENCES**: Finally, when the child has been instructed and trained to do something but chooses not to do so, we move into the correction phase using consequences.
- **CONNECTION**: Apologies, forgiveness, and reconciliation occur so that connection with your child is restored.

Make Communication Our First Go-To Disciplinary Action

Always start with communication! Communication can be very effective if you learn to *minimize warnings, maximize action!*

I want to be clear—this isn't always the easiest thing to do, nor does it always feel natural. At times, I have been guilty of teaching my child *not* to obey immediately. For example, on more than one occasion, I have told my children to get off the computer and get ready for bed several times—without any response from them. After repeated requests, I finally get frustrated and say, "If you don't get off the computer right now, you will lose all computer time tomorrow."

When this happens, they do get off the computer and get ready for bed, which is the goal. But by allowing them to ignore my first request—and then the second, and then the third, and so on—without any consequence, I have created a pattern of delayed obedience. Instead, I should have explained the expectation and consequence upfront so that this pattern was stopped before I got to the point of exasperation. When done properly, there is only one request; after that, immediate consequence is taken if they do not get off the computer right away to go upstairs and get ready for bed.

It is common for parents to count to three, or five, or 10, or some arbitrary number. However, if you use this method, you are telling your child that she doesn't have to obey you until you get to that number. Often, a child has learned not to respond until the parent gets angry and yells. The pattern creates a situation where anger finally causes both the parent and the child to take action. This is the cycle we would like to avoid; we want to create more accountability with the child and foster a good relationship.

At what point do your kids respond? Do they respond to your words or not until you take action? If you want to change your child's actions, you'll need to take action. Once your children see that you will do what you say and take action soon after you give a directive, you will not need to take that action as often—they will more readily obey your words.

For example, years ago, I couldn't get my children to pick up their Nerf darts. They were always scattered all over my house, and my kids weren't very motivated to pick them up after playing with them, even when I asked them to do so.

So I moved to another strategy. I told my kids that I would pick up any Nerf darts I found, but this time, I would *keep* them. If the kids wanted them back, they would have to pay me a nickel for each one. At first they didn't believe me, but I followed through on my actions: I picked them up when I saw them on the floor and put them away in my personal stash. Over time, they had fewer and fewer Nerf darts to play with.

Eventually, they became desperate and decided they needed to buy back the darts from me; they had to spend quite a bit of their allowance money by that point! It was amazing how much better they were at picking up their darts after that. Whenever they started to slip and would fail to pick them up after playing with them, I only had to give them a simple reminder of what would happen if *I* picked them up instead, and they would get right on that. My words meant something because I took action, and they knew what the consequence would be.

No one wants to feel blind-sided, so communicating first gives an opportunity to clarify your request and determine whether the child understood the instruction when we originally gave it—it may be that their disobedience stems from a misunderstanding of the directive. When a child misbehaves, start by asking questions: "What is our rule? What did I ask you to do?" From there, you will be able to discern your next step: Did the child not understand? Not hear? Need coaching or a consequence? It may be resolved with the discussion or you may need to move to a consequence.

Sometimes, it's a matter of making sure the child is listening. There have been times when I have yelled down the stairs for a teen to do something, but they did not hear me because they had headphones on. I was frustrated that they didn't come up and respond, but in reality, I failed in my communication because I was too lazy to go downstairs and talk to them directly.

At other times, it's a matter of making sure the child heard *and* understood. There have been occasions when I have jumped to conclusions and gotten all bent out of shape—but if I had asked questions first, I would have learned either that the child did not understand what I meant or I myself did not understand the situation.

For example, years ago I got an email that our family's cell phone usage had exceeded our plan because of excessive use by our older sons. I didn't know *anything* about our cell phone plans, but I was angry about the extra charges, and so I told the teens who went over that they would have to pay the overage. But after talking with Dave and my sons, I found out that the phone plan my older boys had at that time was different than the phone plan my other teenagers had because the options had changed over the years. My older boys did not realize how limited their phone plan was at that time; they actually *hadn't* used it a lot, but it had added up—hence the overage. They had no idea, and I overreacted. Talk first—don't react.

There will be times when communication will not prevent misbehavior and you will have to move to another level of discipline. But ideally, clear communication can prevent misbehavior and solve the situation right away. There have been many times when I have asked my children to stop doing something, and they have, and that is the end of the problem, with no further need for discipline. Trust me—it is nice when this works and works often.

It will take time, and you will have to follow through with consequences several times, but eventually the clear communication can be very effective. If you haven't been good at following through with consequences in the past, it will take several times following through with consequences for your children to understand that you really mean what you say. Our words need to have meaning and follow through—all the time.

Communication: Not Just Your Words

It's great to talk about communication, but we won't be as effective in it if we don't actually understand what it is. So what is communication? Quite simply, it's exchanging thoughts or ideas. But communication is a lot more than just words. There are actually three components to communication: what you say, how you say it, and the non-verbal cues you use as you interact. You need to be aware and attentive to all aspects of communication, because we are telling our children a lot—much more than the words we are speaking.

What you say
· Words
· Meaning

Non-Verbal
· Eye contact
· Posture
· Gestures
· Facial Expression

How you say it
· Visual, Auditory, Kinesthetic
· Pitch
· Pace
· Volume
· Emotion

All components must be taken into account to communicate meaning. If words are interpreted without attention to the pitch, volume, and emotion of the words, as well as the speaker's posture and the situation in which the words are given, you may end up in a scene like the one in the movie *My Cousin Vinny*, where the sheriff gets a "confession" out of the character Bill. During an interrogation by the sheriff, Bill is asked when he shot the clerk. Bill is confused and shocked and asks, "I shot the clerk?" Later, in the courtroom where the sheriff is speaking at Bill's trial, he is reading the so-called confession, and doing so with completely different intonations. Instead of "I shot the clerk?" the sheriff reads it as if Bill said, "I shot the clerk." Those same words have completely different meanings when given different verbal cues, intonation, and context.[37]

In our family context, misreading of verbal cues and context may not land us in court on a murder charge, but it can still cause plenty of problems. So often, we don't pay attention to how we are communicating with our children. Our attitude, tone, and posture might not match our words, and so we may be conveying a different message to our children than what we are saying. Being able to recognize when this happens is vital in our parenting—we need to make sure all our cues match our words so that the meaning we intend to convey is communicated.

Have you ever watched a parent who was disappointed with a child in public? You can see the emotion in both the parent and the child. The parent's face and body are filled with anger and tension; the scowl, gestures, volume, and pitch are all very obvious. The embarrassment and sadness in the child are evident. Clearly, words are only a small part of this exchange. Is this the kind of vibe you want to give your child?

Yes, it is easy to get frustrated with our children, but we want to communicate that we love them *no matter what*. This needs to ring clearly through your words, actions, gestures, posture, pitch, and so on—especially when you are angry. Remember, we are frustrated with the *behavior*, but we love the child.

Three Forms of Communication

1. **WHAT YOU SAY.** What you say includes both the verbalized words and their meanings. It is important to speak clearly and directly; remember that we can't read minds, nor should we expect our children to be able to.

   Importantly, this also requires us to listen! We shouldn't be talking 90 percent of the time. Who likes to be talked at? If we spent 90 percent of the time listening to our kids, we would have much clearer communication and understanding. This becomes more and more critical as your child gets older. Kids, and especially teens, have thoughts, ideas, opinions, and issues they are wrestling with. We need to take the time to stop what we are doing, look into their eyes, and really listen to what they have to say. That doesn't mean we allow manipulation and begging from our kids, but we must first listen to their point of view and then make our decisions. We also need to wisely choose our words in our response.

2. **HOW YOU SAY IT.** Use a firm voice, but not a harsh tone. A child needs to know that you mean what you are saying, but you must avoid being loud, harsh, and angry in your tone. Have you noticed that often when we're angry, our voices get louder, higher, and faster? Sometimes, we even *accentuate. each. word.* It takes intention, work, and, in my opinion, prayer, to develop self-control in this area. It isn't only the words we say but how we say them that is important.

3. **NON-VERBAL COMMUNICATION.**

   EYE CONTACT is so important in communication. Get at your child's level, look directly into her eyes, and ask her to look at you as well. This shows the other person that she is important, that she has your attention, and that you want hers. With many kids, just getting their attention and having them look at you is extremely helpful in getting a response to your words. Many kids get so immersed in their play, game, computer, or TV, they don't even hear what you are saying. Once you have their attention, your words will be more effective. For some kids, this is easy; for others, this is a real challenge.

When a set of my twins were younger, they would do the silent treatment and sulk if they were frustrated. One way they showed defiance was to look away and refuse to acknowledge I was talking with them. Dave and I know that this is not a good coping strategy, nor will it help them with relationships in the future. We have had to work on having them look at us when we are speaking to them. We talk about using words and letting us know what the problem is so we can resolve the situation. It has not been easy, but as they have gotten older, they have improved in this area.

SMILE! Smiling is contagious; it is difficult for another person to frown when someone smiles at them! Smiling makes us feel better; it releases serotonin, which gives us a feeling of happiness. Smiling makes us more attractive and competent. And who doesn't want that?! Be intentional about smiling, and encourage your children to do the same; see how the mood in your house changes.[38]

The Importance of Word Choice

While the majority of our communication is not done with words, the choice of the words we do use can make a *huge* difference. We need to think intentionally about what we are saying. Remember, we want to have clear communication. Here are some important tips as you consider your word choice:

1. **BE DECISIVE/AUTHORITATIVE; DON'T STATE A WISH WHEN YOU NEED TO STATE A COMMAND.** Don't say, "I think you should go to bed." "I wish you would be quiet." Instead, you should say, "Go up and get your pajamas on now, and I will come up to read your books before bed."

2. **BE SPECIFIC.** Don't say vague statements like, "Shape up." Instead, say, "Stop bothering your brother by making that noise."

3. **DON'T COUNT, CAJOLE, OR COAX.** Don't say, if you don't get off the computer, I am going to count to 10; 1...2...3... Say, "It is time to get off the computer now."

4. **AVOID RHETORICAL QUESTIONS.** Don't say things like, "Don't you think you should pick up your toys?" Similarly, don't say things that start with phrases like, "Wouldn't you like to," or "How about." Begin requests with very clear words like, "I want you to," "Our rule is," or "I need you to."

5. **STATE YOUR COMMAND *ONCE*.** When you make a request, you should expect your child to make a change in behavior right away. Do not make the request again.

6. **AFTER STATING AN EXPECTATION AND CONSEQUENCE CLEARLY, IF THERE IS NO RESPONSE, FOLLOW THROUGH WITH THE CONSEQUENCE.** Be specific in the actions: "If you can't play nicely together with that toy, I am going to put it away until tomorrow."

7. **FOLLOW THROUGH ON CONSEQUENCES.** Instead of constantly repeating your threat, or making threats you cannot follow through on, only say what you can and will do if the misbehavior continues. Then make sure to follow through on the threat.

8. **KEEP CHOICES OR CONSEQUENCES REALISTIC.** Only choose consequences that you can and will do. Don't say, "If you don't eat your dinner, you are never going to get dessert again," or "You are going to be grounded until next year."[39]

Training Tomorrow's Communicators Today

As we use these communication methods to guide and discipline our children, we must also remember that this will help us train our children how to communicate appropriately into adulthood. If we do this starting when they are young, they will learn how to be polite and respectful to others, because they are learning how to be polite and respectful to you. Our children will learn from our example, but it is something we must also plainly teach.

When I was 30 weeks pregnant with my second set of twins, we moved across the country from the Seattle area to Delaware. Those weeks after the move were extremely chaotic. First, we had to travel across the country by an Amtrak train because that was the only mode of transportation my doctors approved for me. When we arrived in Delaware, we spent several days in a hotel before moving into a house; in that time one son had to visit the ER for stitches. Two weeks after arriving in Delaware, a medical emergency resulted in Luke and Levi being born by emergency C-section. Fortunately, my mom had already been with us to help us through the moving process. For the next four weeks, I spent all day in the NICU with Luke and Levi, while my mom took care of the other six kids at home.

At the time, Sophia was only 15 months old, and her world had turned upside down. By the time Luke and Levi came home from the hospital, she had developed a pattern of screaming every time she wanted something. Needless to say, it was very unpleasant.

As soon as I could be home, I had to address this situation. I began to teach her how to ask when she wanted something and the tone she should use. Since she was one of my late talkers, she couldn't *say* the words, but I knew she could try and use much nicer methods to communicate. It only took a few *weeks* of training, and she became much more pleasant again. Changes often don't happen overnight; be consistent and you will see positive changes over time.

Dave and I have had to work on tone and attitude over the years many times with various children. It is never easy, but we always ask ourselves: Is this the kind of behavior we want them to have as adults? Yes, there are developmental growth phases for every child, but we should not make excuses by stating, "She is only 2," or "He is only 4." Do we want them talking that way at 16? 25? 50?

The Power of Apology

Just as in other areas we've discussed, communication is an area where we will also mess up. Again, it's important to apologize—this, too, is an important aspect of teaching. We are always making our children apologize throughout their days. How many times have you had to tell your child, "Say you're sorry for…"? Yet how often do we adults apologize to our children when we make mistakes?

One of my teenagers was having problems with procrastination. He waited until the very last hours to get his school work done. At the end of the first week of school, he finally sat down at 9:30 p.m. to start a biology assignment that was due at midnight. Many college classes have on-line homework software that requires an access code to do the assignment. When he entered the code, he realized it was the wrong software edition. He couldn't do the assignment, and there were only 2.5 hours left.

It is very frustrating as a parent to have consistently taught strategies for writing out a plan to get homework done ahead of time so that there aren't intense, stressful late nights—and yet time and time again, the same scenario occurred with this son. Dave was pretty frustrated and exasperated by yet another occasion in which our son had waited until the last minute to get his school work done, and he expressed that frustration verbally. After researching the situation, we realized that the correct edition had been ordered, but the seller had sent the wrong one. The correct version could be ordered from the publisher in a few minutes' time, and our son was able to complete the assignment before midnight with a 98 percent grade. But at that moment, it was pretty frustrating and emotions were running high.

After our son completed his assignment and came in to tell us, Dave asked him to stay and chat. He apologized for his reaction and explained all the things that our son was doing well. He also told him that he would be happy to sit down with him again and show him how to write out a daily plan for the semester. You could feel the tensions lift and dissipate after Dave's apology and encouragement. Our frustration over a situation cannot cloud the message that we love and believe in our children.

When we blow it, we need to apologize and restore that relationship. As I've repeated several times, our children need to know we love them, no matter what. Apologizing to them when we've done something wrong is an important way to do this. Not only does it set the relationship right, but it provides an important lesson for our kids. Let's set the example when that situation arises.

1. In what ways are you communicating well?
2. What could you improve upon?
3. Think about a recent scenario with your child. What was the pattern from misbehavior to action? When does your child change the behavior? Is it when you are using words or when you take action?

4Cs

CHAPTER 8

Spilled Milk and What to do About It: Natural and Logical Consequences

PARENTING POINT: Turning messes into successes

"One morning Hi told me to catch up another horse for a couple of days, because we were going to 'learn' Sky to stand ground-tied. Hi saddled him, and put on a bridle with short reins and a big rowel in the bit. The rowel was so big that the colt could hardly close his mouth without having it cut against his tongue and the roof of his mouth. After that, Hi got a long iron picket pin with an eye-loop at the top. Then we led Sky high up into the canyon, drove the picket pin clear down to the eye, and ground-tied him within twenty feet of the brook.

There was good grass around the picket, but he couldn't eat it with the rowel bit in his mouth. And every time he tried to take a step forward or back, the bit would cut the rowel into the roof of his mouth or against his tongue. I got mad about that, and told Hi it was a dirty thing to do, and there ought to be some easier way of teaching a horse. He said, 'Yep, they's easier ways, and it would be easier for him to forget. The lessons you remember longest are the ones that hurt you the most when you learn 'em. Do you follow what I'm tryin' to tell you?'"

(From *Little Britches: Father and I Were Ranchers* by Ralph Moody.)[40]

This passage from *Little Britches: Father and I Were Ranchers* describes a different time and place, but its truth still stands: It is through trial and struggle that we learn the deepest lessons.

We're inspired by stories of struggle. When we read books or watch movies, we are drawn in by the stories of the hardships the characters overcome; we are fascinated by seeing how those struggles shape them. Often there is a backstory of overcoming hardship after hardship, rejection after rejection, before success is finally realized. Perseverance and determination—these are the qualities we need to develop in our children so that they, too, can succeed.

Yet many parents do everything in their power to protect their children from any misfortune, pain, or disappointment. Unfortunately, this "helicopter parenting" has resulted in young adults who are anxious, depressed, overwhelmed by responsibility, and unable to solve basic life challenges. Colleges have been swamped by an increasing number of students who are having difficulties with depression and anxiety, or who are unable to navigate any challenge that comes up, whether academic or social. Parents and students are calling the president of the college—or even 911—for things they should be able to solve on their own. For example, two students called 911 because they saw a mouse in their off-campus apartment and then needed counseling for this event. College students are having difficulty handling relationship issues or poor grades without feeling like the world is ending and are taking no personal responsibility, but blaming others instead.[41] Doing things for your children that they should do for themselves leaves them incapable of resolving situations on their own.

We need to change our way of thinking. Instead of overprotecting our children—or, on the opposite end of the spectrum, condemning our children for mistakes—we need to look at mistakes and failures as opportunities to learn life's lessons. Coach your children through their mistakes and challenges by teaching *them* to learn problem-solving. This will turn messes into successes. Using natural and logical consequences does that! Don't underestimate the invaluable wisdom they will learn through their mistakes if those experiences are viewed through the proper lens.

As we have discussed previously with the 4 Cs, it is important to remember to communicate first and then take the time to coach your children. But if you have done your teaching and training and your child has not responded, you now have to decide which consequence to use. In the remainder of this chapter, we will explore natural and logical consequences.

Natural Consequences

Natural consequences is shorthand for a method of discipline in which a parent *doesn't* step in; instead, she or he simply lets the natural effects of the child's choice take place. This is a method we use quite often in our house, so I have plenty of examples to cite!

When one of my kids forgets goggles for swim team practice, they will have to work out a solution, because I am going to allow the natural consequences to occur. They can try to borrow spare goggles from a sibling or a friend, or use one from the lost-and-found bin; otherwise, they swim without goggles for that practice. My kids hear their friends complain regularly, "My mom forgot my goggles; my mom forgot my towel; my mom forgot…" Even at their young age, my kids are shocked at the lack of personal responsibility and tell their friends to pack their own bag.

By constantly doing things *for* your kids, you prevent them from learning such life skills as planning ahead, being responsible, or accepting natural consequences. Instead, they are learning to blame someone else. How many adults out there continue to blame someone else for everything that goes wrong in their lives? Allow your children to learn from these experiences.

Another example from our family: If a child repeatedly forgets to take a lunch, they go without for that day; we do not bring one to them. I was recently talking to one of my older sons, and we were laughing about this. He said he has repeatedly forgotten his lunch when he goes to work, so he still goes without lunch many times as an adult. He has written notes in several locations and on his door to help him remember! Some of these tendencies follow us into adulthood, but we need to develop our own strategies and continue to take responsibility.

If one of my children loses money, the money is gone; he or she has to re-earn it. This has happened many times in my house. I heard one mom say that she doesn't let her kids have the money they have earned; instead, she keeps it all and has a chart stating how much money each child has. She keeps track of the money and deducts it from a chart when they spend some. This takes away the child's responsibility and their opportunity to handle and manage money. Dave remembers—very vividly—the day he left his wallet, brimming with bills from his cashed paycheck, on the top of his car after filling up with gas. He was in college; that money was hard-earned and extremely important. He has never placed his wallet on the top of the car again. It stinks to lose money, but you want to teach your children to keep track of their cash carefully, as well as how to cope with the loss and go on.

If a child refuses to wear his coat to school on a cold day, he is cold during the day. Most of us have encountered this battle at some time or another. It is freeing not to engage in the battle; allow the natural consequence to happen.

If a child didn't do her school work, allow her to have the consequences of the grade. One year, my 16-year-old forgot to do an online test for one of his community college classes. He was sitting in class when he realized he had forgotten it, so he did it as soon as he got home. He got 100 percent on the test, but it was two hours too late, so he got a zero; that was the teacher's policy. That zero sent my son's grade from a solid A to barely a C. Understandably, he was upset about it. He emailed his teacher asking if there was anything he could do to make up points, and received the depressing news that nothing could be done to change the zero.

When I learned about the situation, I expressed empathy and told him that it was a bummer, but I also encouraged him to do the best he could from that point forward. We also talked about the fact that it was going to be okay; it was disappointing, but life would continue. I thought it was a tough policy, but I left the issue in my son's hands to talk to the teacher. He learned to work through it himself. He also learned that the world didn't end and that life was going to be okay, even though his grade took a hit. He worked very hard and was able to pull his grade up to a B by the end of the semester. He was also much more attentive to when assignments and tests were due. Had his teacher been lenient, the experience would not have made the same impact that the harsh reality had.

If a child is refusing to get up and get ready for school, allow the natural consequence to occur. It's common for a parent to go to great lengths to get a child to school on time. Instead, it would be better to use communication and coaching to teach the child how to use an alarm clock starting at a young age. Then explain what time the child needs to get up in order to have enough time to get ready for school and eat breakfast. Then it is up to the child. If he is late, he comes to school late and accepts whatever consequence the school gives out. Over time, a child will learn to take responsibility, and you can eliminate the battle in which *you* try to get the child ready and out the door. Leave it in your child's lap, so he can learn how to take responsibility. (Of course, this does require some discernment; I do understand this can't always be done if, for example, that consequence would also jeopardize a parent's ability to get to work.)

When our kids get jobs as teenagers, they are responsible for keeping track of the days and times they work, getting their availability to their bosses, and finding replacements if they can't work a shift. They also have to make sure they set their alarm to get there on time. It is their responsibility. Our kids have had to miss fun events in order to work because they were not proactive in finding a replacement.

Ultimately, your children will have to function independently as adults; it is important to give them as much responsibility as possible when they are young so they learn these skills. Allowing natural consequences is key! My children have overslept and have been late to work, and they have had to deal with their bosses in those situations—just as they will in their adulthood.

Of course, we do have to make sure to use common sense when deciding to use natural consequences. Don't allow natural consequences to happen if it would cause injury or harm to your child. For example, with a child, you must intervene to prevent them from getting burned or from drowning; in those instances, you *don't* allow natural consequences to occur!

Logical Consequences

When using logical consequences, the parent creates a plan so a negative consequence occurs that is logically related to the misbehavior.

For example, if a child writes on the wall, she has to clean the marks off the wall. There is an apparent relationship between the behavior and the consequence.

Logical consequences benefits:

1. It is effective with preschoolers through teenagers.
2. It teaches responsibility.
3. It establishes parental authority in a healthy and effective way, weakening any struggles for power with children—especially with strong-willed children.
4. It can change current and future behavior.
5. It addresses the *behavior* instead of shaming the child.[42]

However, developing logical consequences takes practice and thought. Here, too, our family has many examples of logical consequences in action.

When a child spills something, I teach him or her how to clean it; the action is logically related to the situation. It's safe to say that spills are frustrating. However, spills are usually unintentional; the reality is that we *all* spill sometimes. Instead of getting angry, teach your child how he or she can clean it up. It teaches them how to do life. It isn't something to get bent out of shape over; just fix the situation and go on.

Unfortunately, I have had a lot of experience with poop in underwear. We have always used the logical consequence of having the child clean it up. Our goal is that having to clean it up themselves will be a deterrent from doing it again. When Katie was potty-training, I told her that she would have to clean out her underwear, and she very cheerfully agreed to do so. I walked her through how to do this. When she was done cleaning them out, she said, "That was fun. I like cleaning my underwear!" *Not* the response I was hoping for, but at least she was taking responsibility! It also keeps me from being angry at having to clean out messy underwear. But this does require help and training with supervision and good handwashing (it can double as an introduction to the importance of good hygiene, too!).

If the children are fighting over a toy and can't work it out themselves, I usually take the toy away. Similarly, if the children refuse to clean up toys, I either hide the toys and do not allow them to play with them, or I will give the toys away. With this training, I use good communication to let my children know ahead of time that I will give a certain toy away if they don't pick up their toys within a certain amount of time. It is best to set a specific time limit and then use a timer. Try to keep it concise; kids are easily distracted and need get-it-done-now training. If you say, "Clean up these toys today, or I will give them away," it is less likely to get done than if you say, "I am going to set the timer for 15 minutes. Let's see how fast you can get these picked up." Usually, by creating this habit, you won't get to the point of having to give things away. But if you do get to this point (and I have on several occasions), you *have* to give them away. Don't choose this consequence if you can't follow through.

It can be hard to do this—especially if *you* were the one who paid for the toy—but it will be worth it. After I gave away a couple of toys, it didn't take long before my kids started picking toys up.

There are a lot of other practical logical consequences that we utilize in our family:

- When a child breaks a toy, they don't have that toy anymore; they can save up their own money to buy a new one. If they maliciously break another person's thing, they will have to earn money to replace it.
- If the kids don't get their chores or schoolwork done, they cannot play with friends.
- If a teen is not showing responsibility in his driving, he will have limitations placed on his driving—or perhaps will not be able to drive at all—until things change.
- If a child is spending too much time on the phone or gaming device, the device will be taken away for a period of time.

Natural consequences are easier to use because they happen organically; you let the results of a choice happen and allow the child to feel the inconvenience, pain, or work of his/her choices. But logical consequences take thought and creativity. In my experience, it is best to think through common situations and discern what the most logical consequence would be. Do not forget about the importance of communication; in order for a logical consequence to be the most effective, you need to talk through the consequence with your child ahead of time.

For example, when I first used the tactic of giving away toys that were not put away, I told my children, "It is important for you to learn how to pick up your toys. When I ask you to clean them up, you start complaining and find many excuses and end up not picking them up. I want you to learn to appreciate and take care of the amazing toys you have. So the next time I ask you to pick them up, I am going to set a timer for 30 minutes. When the timer goes off, the toys left out will go in my give-away box to be given to other boys and girls to enjoy. Do you understand?" Once you have clearly explained the consequences, remember to follow through with what you have stated.

This is not easy to do. That is why I have found these principles from the book *Discipline Them Love Them*[43] to be helpful and encouraging:

1. *If you are angry, you will not be able to use logical consequences effectively.*
2. *Communicate with the child first. Tell the child the logical consequence that will take place if the misbehavior happens again.*
3. *The consequence must be negative to the child. What is negative to one child is not necessarily negative to another child. You need to know each child.*
4. *The consequence must be logically related to the misbehavior. In other words, there must a relationship between what the child did and the consequence that the parent plans.*
5. *The child must have the freedom to make his own choice. Do not use logical consequences if you get mad when the child chooses the consequence; then you don't really want him to have a choice. A strong-willed child will test you to see if he really does have a choice. You cannot interfere with the child's decision making. Give a child the freedom to "blow it," because it is in these circumstances that she will learn responsibility. It is better that she learns to be responsible now rather than in adulthood. **The only way to teach responsibility is to give responsibility.***
6. *Stay out of the way and let the consequence do the correcting. Let the child take the consequences of his action; do not rescue him. If you find that you are emotionally involved, think about the positive growth and responsible behavior that is developing in him.*
7. *Be sure that the task involved is within the child's capabilities and the consequences are reasonable. She may be capable, but not experienced, in doing the task. If so, lovingly teach the child how to do the task while she is doing it.*

Now you may be thinking, "This sounds good in theory, but what do I do if I can't think of a natural or logical consequence?" In my own parenting, I find it best and most effective when I have a natural or logical consequence, but there are times when I don't have this. In those situations, Dave and I take away something meaningful to that child, like desserts, computer time, or time with friends. For my younger children, we have occasionally used time outs as well, but having the connection/reconciliation component is crucial. With most of my children, these techniques work very well. The child has a consequence and eventually decides he would rather just follow the rules and guidelines than have to deal with the consequence. This has been extremely effective in our family.

Working with Strong-willed Children

In an ideal world, when our children disobeyed, we would only have to correct them once. We would know exactly what to say and do, and they would respond to our instruction with respect and immediate obedience because they understand the value of what we're saying. What a dream!

Reality is different. As I mentioned earlier, many of the techniques we have been discussing work well in our family for much of the time. However, given the number of children I have, I have some who are *very* strong-willed, and it has been more difficult to discipline them. It is so hard to have a strong-willed child who challenges thing after thing, day after day. One thing isn't right, and the next several hours are spent trying to recover from the fallout. It is exhausting and can be disheartening as well.

However, I truly believe that the same stubborn traits that can make parenting difficult can also be some of my children's best traits. Perseverance and determination—these are the qualities we need to develop in our children so they, too, can succeed. This is why we must be committed to working on a child's issues and continue our calling to parent faithfully with love and discipline. Don't give up. As that child grows older, we want her to be strong and able to know right from wrong so she can stand up for what she believes in.

Major on the Majors; Minor on the Minors[44]

When we are having difficulties in parenting our children, we must remember to *major on the majors and minor on the minors*. Often, the majors are heart issues like disrespect or dishonesty, where the minors are more behavioral adjustments. Don't make a massive deal about something that just isn't a big deal. For example, if your daughter wants to wear cowboy boots with a non-western dress (like mine does), let her. As parents, we feel embarrassed when our kids are mismatched, but it is okay to let our kids make choices. That is a minor thing to let go; don't nitpick everything the child isn't doing right. If, however, it is a disrespect issue, where a child rolls his eyes, deliberately looks away, and/or has a clearly disdainful or rebellious attitude, that is a major thing and will need to be addressed. Also, when kids are lying or refusing to take responsibility for their actions, you have to deal with that.

When I first started teaching parenting classes, I was struggling with frequent and exhausting conflicts with my younger set of twins. They were expert fit throwers; over the color of their cup, which shirt they would wear, or a magnitude of other things. I prayed nearly daily for years about these matters and continued to use these skills in my parenting, and slowly things started to improve. Now, at 11 years old, they are kind and delightful boys. They have matured, and the battles that we fought so often when they were younger are rare. When I went to see my son, Ben, his wife, Ariana, and their new baby a couple of years ago, Luke made them Valentine's Day cards and a card for the baby that I brought with me. When Ben and Ariana opened them up, there were five dollars—a week of Luke's allowance—in each card. At Christmas a few years ago, Luke made a thoughtfully drawn picture for each sibling, for his grandparents, and for Dave and I, and enclosed one dollar in each one; that same Christmas, Levi gave all he had to Dave and me—almost fifty dollars. (Dave got a larger share, but I agree, Dave is pretty great!) The twins' compassion and their "give all I have to others" mentality bring tears to my eyes. Seeing the young men they are becoming has made those years of struggle and exhaustion meaningful.

Our kids have to know that we believe in them, even when there are frustrating battles. In the midst of conflict, we must remind them that we love them, no matter what, and that we do what we do in order to guide them into adulthood. We are called to parent faithfully through the good times and the rough times.

This week, brainstorm about common situations in your home and consider what natural and logical consequences you can start to implement. Keep your thoughts on the 4 Cs: Communicate, Coach, Consequence, and Connection. Our children are going to make mistakes and struggle along the way just as we do. Remember: **VIEW YOUR CHILD'S MISTAKES AND STRUGGLES AS OPPORTUNITIES FOR THEM TO GROW, AND TURN THE MESS INTO A SUCCESS!**

1. List some recurrent struggles you are having with your kid(s).
2. What natural consequences could you implement?
3. What logical consequences could you implement?

CHAPTER 9

Uncovering the Truth About Rewards

PARENTING POINT: Praise God, encourage kids.[45]
Kevin Leman

 $ for grades

Candy or treats if child behaves

 **$ for scoring during sporting games**

Trophies and certificates for participating

Formal graduation ceremonies preschool, K, 5th and 8th grade

Offering rewards to get kids to do something is a common parenting strategy. Kids are also bombarded by rewards at school, sports, and clubs. There are formal graduation events for preschool, kindergarten, and all stages through a child's education. Parents give their children candy or some other item if they behave in the store, offer money for grades or goals made, or an array of other rewards for behaving a certain way. Many parents want their kid to be "happy," so on the surface, the idea of "if you do this, you will get that" seems like a logical tactic. It has become so commonplace that earning a "reward" has lost the specialness of some big accomplishment. Every kid gets a trophy for participating in sports. Prizes are given for reading books. But what is the true impact of giving children all these rewards? Do they help, or do they hinder?

Even though it seems like a simple solution to create elaborate charts and reward systems to make our children behave the way we want, we must look at what the research shows. You may want to save the money spent on stars, coins, stickers, candy, or that basket of trinkets for the child to "buy" at your "store." Although B.F. Skinner did extensive research on the effects of rewards and negative reinforcement on the behavior of rats, we must be cautious about expecting the same results with humans who have much higher thinking and reasoning abilities.

How well do rewards work for children? In what situation should they be used? Do rewards encourage kids to be self-motivated to work hard? Do rewards enhance enthusiasm for learning and being creative? Does a constant stream of rewards make them feel better about themselves, or not? Hundreds of research studies have been done on rewards and motivation, and the results are *not* what you might think.

According to "Rewards and Praise: The Poisoned Carrot—The Natural Child Project website,"[46] there are many studies that show that children perform worse when they expect or anticipate rewards. One study revealed that giving a child money for grades decreased the student's performance. Other studies showed that rewards suppressed students' creativity—they avoided challenges and only did the minimum required to get the reward. Other research shows that when rewards are offered, often the child's interest or liking of the task decreases.[47]

When to Use or Not Use Rewards

When rewards are given for actions that don't require much thinking, like attendance or following a dress code, incentives seem to work. However, if rewards are given for grades or higher-thinking tasks, incentives have the opposite effect. For example, if there is a large reward for getting straight As on a report card, the child may think that is too much work and unattainable, and her grades may fall lower rather than rise. That reward can make her think, "Why should I even bother, since I will never get that reward anyway?"

Borrowing a technique from Edward Deci, Oprah Winfrey staged an experiment in 1996 and asked Alfie Kohn, an author and speaker on human behavior, education, and parenting, to come onto her show to explain the results.[48] Twenty teenagers were invited into an office building, one at a time, and were greeted by someone who pretended she worked for a toy company. Each teen was invited to evaluate some new puzzles. Half the teens were promised a reward of $5 for each puzzle they tested. After the playing and evaluating were done, each child was left alone in the room for a few minutes and secretly videotaped. It turned out that every one of the 10 kids who had participated without any mention of payment played with one of the puzzles when the formal testing period was over and no one was around. But of the 10 kids who had been rewarded for participating, nine did not touch a puzzle again. The mere offer of the reward changed the teen's thinking about the puzzles from fun to *not* fun as soon as they were paid to play with them.

After looking at hundreds of studies similar to this one, Kohn published his findings as *Punished by Rewards: The Trouble with Gold Stars, Incentive Plans, A's, Praise, and Other Bribes.*[49] He found that rewards offered only temporary obedience and inferior work. Also, rewards decreased interest in whatever task people were being rewarded to do.

Motivation and Rewards

In order to better understand this, we have to understand *motivation*. Motivation is what drives us to do something. First we have motivation; then we act. That motivation may come from our belief that a particular action is the right thing to do; it may be something that makes us feel good. We may do something because we derive pleasure from doing it, like painting, building something, or baking. This is called *intrinsic motivation.*

We might also be motivated by a tangible reward we will receive, like a paycheck, a first-place ribbon, or a prize. We may also do something because we're avoiding a negative reward. For example, a student may study hard for a test to avoid failing a class or getting in trouble with his parents. This is *extrinsic motivation.* Whether intrinsic or extrinsic, the motivation is our impetus, what gives us a reason to do things. First there is motivation; then the action is done.

On the other hand, a reward is something that is received *after* the action is done. As with motivations, there are *intrinsic* rewards and *extrinsic* rewards.

Intrinsic rewards refer to the feeling a person gets when they do something—a sense of accomplishment and satisfaction. As we will soon learn, these feelings are almost always more satisfying and effective than extrinsic rewards.

Extrinsic rewards are external rewards given by others.

There are three types of extrinsic rewards:

- Affection or social rewards: These are words or touch that provide encouragement and support: "I love you," "I am proud of you," "Thank you," or a hug.
- Attention or activity rewards: These are activities that a person deems "fun" or "rewarding," such as having a friend over, spending time with mom or dad playing a game, going to a movie, or going out to eat.
- Physical rewards: These are material items, like ice cream, candy, soda, toys, clothes, or money.[50]

The Parenting Goal: Developing Intrinsic Motivation

As we have seen, material rewards are not often helpful in parenting our children. Ultimately, what we want is for our children to be self-motivated in their work; we do not want them to be doing things just for a reward. We also don't want rewards to take away the enjoyment they derive from doing things. Our children—and our families—will be most successful when we train them to develop their intrinsic motivation so they do something because they *want* to, not to gain some tangible thing.

In order to do this, we must understand the three components to intrinsic motivation: autonomy, mastery, and purpose.

Autonomy

Autonomy is the urge to direct our own lives. People thrive when they have choices to pursue what they desire and have the ability to apply their skills. Some of the most innovative companies embrace opportunities to increase intrinsic motivation by allowing employees to spend part of their work time pursuing projects that interest them—even if it's not directly tied to their specific role at the company.

In 1993, Microsoft hired many paid experts to create a digital encyclopedia called Encarta, which contained more than 62,000 articles by 2008. Similarly, in 2001, Larry Sanger and Jimmy Wales used another model to create an online encyclopedia, one people were intrinsically motivated to work on not because they were paid for it—most were not, in fact—but because of their passion for a topic.[51]

At first glance, we would assume that the best encyclopedia would be the one created by the paid experts, right? But those intrinsically motivated, unpaid people were the creators and contributors to Wikipedia, which at the time of writing this has more than 5,396,444 articles, and adds, on average, about 800 new articles each day!

How does this relate to raising our children? When Josh, my oldest son, was in second grade, he was assigned to read one chapter per week of a specific book. He was scolded if he read ahead of the class, because every student needed to be at the same point in the book for discussion. It was torture for him to drag the book out for months, but he would have loved the book had he been able to read the whole book in an afternoon. How much more motivated is a child who can choose the topic of the book and can read as much on the topic as he or she desires? That loss of autonomy squelched Josh's love of reading that particular book.

Unfortunately, many reading incentive programs have the opposite of their intended outcome. On the surface, it seems like a great idea to offer pizza or prizes to motivate children to read more—and at first, kids did in fact increase the number of books they read. However, reading became something to do to get the reward, so shorter, large printed books were the most sought after. Even the Accelerated Reader program, which makes kids pick books from a list and take a quiz to get their reward, did not work as intended. The students often skimmed to find key points needed to answer the quiz rather than reading with engagement and enjoyment. The enthusiasm for voluntary reading dropped significantly, and there was no increase in comprehension or vocabulary. If there was no reward, there was no reading, because reading no longer felt enjoyable.[52][53]

Using intrinsic motivation is effective in more areas of education beyond reading comprehension. It is not uncommon for kids to have art assignments where they are told to color the picture or make the project exactly as the teacher did. This leaves no room for autonomy and creativity. To increase the child's intrinsic motivation instead, supply an assortment of paper, crayons, paint, scissors, and various craft supplies, and tell them, "Create whatever you want."

When my children are passionate about learning something, I have tried to open the doors for them to explore that topic through books, hands-on exploration, or field trips. This can be more difficult if a child does not have a clearly defined area of interest, or if her interest is in something that can be difficult to open doors for because of finances, location limitations, time, and the like. But when additional learning experiences are available, remember communication is important— encourage the child to try different things, and ask them later how they enjoyed that activity or project. If there are constraints to helping your child explore something that interests them, try to come up with creative ways to allow them to learn. Libraries and community centers are great resources for books and activities, and there is much that can be learned and studied through online resources.

It is also important to keep in mind that your child's interests will likely change over time; continue to encourage them through those changes. Josh was very interested in working at NASA when he was young. He read and explored whatever he wanted about space. We frequented the Air and Space Museum in Seattle and met Buzz Aldrin at a book signing event. When he was a junior in high school, he took a constitutional law class online, which completely changed his career path. He became passionate about law, government, global economics, world poverty, and modern-day slavery. He taught *me* things I had never known or thought about. He took an economics course and created his own course on global poverty and modern-day slavery during his senior year of high school. He did a summer internship for a nonprofit micro-finance organization that operates in some of the poorest countries in the world. He studied peace and conflict resolution in Belfast, Northern Ireland; he donates regularly to causes he is passionate about; he even ran a marathon in the West Bank in support of peace. By being allowed to follow his passions, Josh has learned far more than if I had adhered to a standard curriculum while home schooling.

Often we find that we are able to help our children receive great satisfaction in exploring their passions and interests while also teaching them to use their talents for different responsibilities around the house. With our 23-year-old, Ben, who loves to build things and is now a mechanical engineer, Dave worked alongside him to teach him how to make things. When we lived in Delaware, Ben designed and constructed a great built-in bench in the kitchen, as well as two amazing step stools for the bathrooms. He spent a summer working in a forge, learning about metals, and then did an internship for a manufacturing company. By being allowed to follow his passions, Ben was able to find work in things he was interested in over the years, which prepared him for his career in manufacturing now.

Sam showed interest in computer programming. By the time he was in ninth grade, he was taking free online programming courses. He is now finishing his bachelor's degree in computer engineering. Jake, my 18-year-old, started showing an interest in computer graphics when he was about 11; he began doing graphic work for online gamers at that time. He just completed his associate's degrees in graphic design and multimedia design and will be transferring to complete his four-year degree this fall. Encouraging each child to pursue his interests through projects, education, or work experience is key for developing intrinsic motivation.

With my younger children, we encourage them to use their gifts and talents to pursue art, building Legos, baking, singing, and anything else they are interested in. One of my sons *loved* dinosaurs at the age of 4. We read and read about dinosaurs for a couple years until he moved on to his next passion. I didn't discourage him when he talked about becoming a paleontologist but allowed him the opportunity to learn what he was interested in. Letting children feel this autonomy to do what they are passionate about increases their intrinsic motivation and opens up a world of possibilities.

Mastery

Mastery is the urge to get better and better at something that matters. Everyone wants to get better at whatever their passion is, whether it is a sport, an instrument, or a job where they want to perform well. Allow opportunities for your kids to practice and explore those areas they are interested in—and, just as importantly, allow opportunities for failure, as it is through overcoming failures that we succeed.

The 2016 Olympics in Rio was particularly special to our family because my kids used to swim on the same team as Cierra Runge, who was in the 4x200 freestyle relay. In an interview, she explained that her Olympic dream started when she watched Olympic swimmers as a 4-year-old and told her mom she wanted to do that. At that point, she started swimming lessons. She had that intrinsic desire to master swimming and realize the dream of going to the Olympics.[54]

It is important that pursuing training in particular skills be child-directed—not what the *parent* wants the child to desire. My mom was a violinist, pianist, and organist, and she wanted all her children to follow the same passion for music. When I was around 4 years old, I started violin and piano lessons. Although I now think the violin is a beautiful instrument and wish I could play well, when I was a child, I had no interest in playing it. I practiced because I had to—not because I wanted to. In fifth grade, the band director started recruiting students to play a variety of instruments; I longed to learn the flute or do percussion. My mom told me, "No." I had to play the violin, in spite of the fact that my heart was not in it. Finally, in junior high, when I came home with a D on my report card in orchestra for not practicing, my mom let me quit. In contrast, my parents let my youngest brother choose his instrument—which ironically happened to be the flute—and he played through high school.

So often, a parent wants their passion to be their child's. But if a child doesn't have the intrinsic motivation, he will not have the heart to master that skill—no matter how many private lessons, camps, coaches, and years are spent practicing that activity. The more a child does it for the parent, the more he or she will resent doing it.

Purpose

Purpose is yearning to do what we do in the service of something larger than ourselves. To feel that intrinsic motivation, we need to believe that it has a purpose—that there is importance to what we are doing.

In a New York Times article from 2007, Barry Schwartz, a Swarthmore College professor, told the story of a situation in Switzerland where well-informed citizens were asked if they were willing to allow a nuclear waste dump in their community. Astonishingly, 50 percent of the citizens said yes. They knew it was dangerous. They thought it would reduce their property values. But it had to go somewhere, and they had responsibilities as citizens.

However, when other people were asked the same question and also offered six weeks' salary as compensation, only 25% agreed to have the waste dump. Once money was offered, the decision involved personal interest; is that amount of money worth having the waste cite nearby?[55]

In 2000, the economists Uri Gneezy and Aldo Rustichini ran an experiment where they announced the imposition of a fine every time parents were late picking up their children from a childcare facility. After the introduction of the fine they observed an *increase* in the number of the parents coming late, a rate twice as high as before the introduction of the fine. No longer did the parents worry about being considerate to the workers. Instead, it became a financial decision: Is the value of the extra personal time greater than the cost of the fine?[56]

When people feel they are doing something altruistic, they are more willing to do that task. When money comes into the picture, that motivation changes from *wanting* to do something because it is the right thing to do into *weighing* the possibilities of what we have to gain or lose.

How does this impact our parenting? By allowing our children the opportunity to do something for the good of our society, they can develop this desire and the good character that undergirds it. If you pay or reward children to do something good, it may take away that effect. Our children need to understand that they are not the center of the universe but that who they are and what their gifts are can positively impact the world around them . . . a true reward.

We encourage our children to begin doing this kind of work from a young age. Below are some ideas that have worked for us.

Encourage them to volunteer at church or some other organization. My daughter, Sophia, 12, is a teacher's helper in children's ministry at church. Sam has also served in various capacities, like AV/tech support during services and special events. He has also been a middle school mentor for many years. Neither one receives external rewards for this work, but instead they find joy and satisfaction in serving.

Lead your children to notice needs they can serve within your neighborhood. When we lived in Delaware, a neighbor down the street lost her husband suddenly at the age of 52. She needed help with yard work, so our family, as well as some other neighbors and extended family, went over to help her out. The little kids, including 3-year-old Katie, picked up black walnuts, filling several buckets, while the older kids did a lot of raking. We worked all morning—not for any extrinsic reward, but to help another person, the importance of which was a lesson I wanted to teach my children. They all got to experience the intrinsic reward of feeling good about helping this widow. (I will dive deeper into this topic in Chapter 12, "Serving Others: The Antidote for Self-centeredness.")

What about social rewards? Of course we need to hug and encourage our children, but we also need to be careful of harmful praise and flattery. Telling a child things like, "You are pretty" is not actually helpful for self-esteem. For example, telling a girl she is pretty can be harmful, because she begins internalizing that she is loved because of her beauty, which will cause her to become more concerned about her looks. This is especially dangerous in today's culture, where many body images young girls see have been altered, slenderized, and touched up, making beauty "standards" unattainable. Children as young as 7 are being treated for eating disorders, and the number of hospitalizations for them is increasing.[57] [58] Boys, too, are affected by this kind of pressure to look and behave a certain way in order to be popular and successful. We need to be especially sensitive to physical praise, and we must balance cultural pressure on external beauty by encouraging our children on their work ethic, their kindness, and other similar traits.

Like material rewards, praise for things like looks or athletic ability or artistic ability conditions children to seek approval, reassurance, and recognition of those traits, which can then lead to depression if that approval isn't gained or a child is struggling in something at which they usually excel.

This means we should focus on actual accomplishments and effort. For my children who are on the swim team, I try to offer positive encouragement on their accomplishments by saying such things as, "You have been working very hard during swim practice, and during that race, you swam two seconds faster!"

It is also best to focus on the *child's* sense of accomplishment rather than training them only to seek praise or rewards. To do this, we should ask questions like, "How did you feel about that race?" If a child is showing you artwork, instead of saying, "You are quite an artist," say, "Tell me about your picture. What is your favorite part about it?" This helps them learn to internalize their thoughts, feelings, and accomplishments, as well as trains them to be articulate about their work. Be specific in your encouragement. When commenting on a piece of art, say things like, "I like the colors you chose." Instead of telling a young girl, "You look pretty today," say, "I really like the way you layered those shirts. It matches very well and will keep you warm, too."

This is just as true when we talk about our children's intelligence. It can be common to hear, "You're so smart!" When a child who has been told this messes up, he then thinks, "Oh, no, I am not smart." Thus, the praise of their intelligence can backfire, lessening their desire to take chances for fear of making a mistake. Wanting to keep the image of being smart, they avoid trying things they may fail at or decrease their work effort.

Instead, we want to encourage our kids that it is through mistakes, hard work, and failure that we learn. The most successful people in the world have become successful precisely because of repeated failures.

Carol Dweck, a psychologist and one of the leading experts on motivation, has done extensive research on this topic of praising intelligence; I highly recommend reading more of her work on this subject to fully grasp its importance. Start by reading the article, "How Not to Talk to Your Kids: the inverse power of praise," for an excellent summary. The most important take-away is to praise *effort*, not intelligence.[59] There is a link to this article on my website, www.parentingsensibly.com, under parenting resources.

Our kids do need our love and encouragement, but we must also remember that it is important to think about how we state things so that our children feel *true* encouragement. Instead of subconsciously implying to a child, "I have to do something that pleases Mom," or "I need to look a certain way," our words should show that we delight in seeing our children enjoy what they are doing in their pursuit of their passions.

When Rewarding is Okay

Though our goal is to build our children's intrinsic motivation, it is fine to give occasional *spontaneous* rewards when they have done something we want to honor and acknowledge. When we were visiting my parents in Arizona several years ago, Josh and Ben spent most of a day helping

Dave replace all the door knobs, handles, and lock sets in their house. After all the work was done, my dad insisted on paying the boys. It was a way to say, "Thank you," for all the work they had done and was an unexpected reward. When kids help me bake cookies, I usually reward them with an extra cookie or two for all the work they did to help make them.

In moments like this, spontaneous rewards can be fun and don't negatively affect a child's intrinsic motivation—and research backs this up. There was an interesting study done on 51 preschoolers who loved to draw.[60] The researchers wanted to see what happened to the children's love of drawing if a reward was given. The children were randomly assigned to one of three groups:

- *Reward*: These children were told they would receive a certificate with a gold seal and a ribbon for participating.
- *Surprise reward*: This group was not told about any reward, but were surprised with the same reward as above after they participated.
- *No reward.*

Each child spent six minutes in a separate room where they could draw. At the end of the time, they were given the reward as promised, or as a surprise, or no reward at all, depending on which group they were in. Over the next several days, the researchers observed the children in their classroom behind one-way glass, noting how many minutes the child chose to draw on their own.

Those who had received the expected reward drew half as much as those who received no reward or a surprise reward. All these children previously showed great interest in drawing, but after expecting a reward, their interest in spontaneously drawing dropped significantly. Something the child had previously found enjoyable now became less fun once they were told they would receive a reward for doing it. The take-away is this: giving rewards changes one's perception of a task so that the task is viewed more negatively. So occasional, spontaneous, *unexpected* rewards are fine, but please do not use rewards in a "do this and I will give you that" framework.

Bucking the system

Does this mean that there is no place for rewards at all in our parenting? Not necessarily. I think there is a time and a place for rewards. Rewards can be effective for a limited number of situations. They could be used in the *training* level. For example, in potty-training, it may be helpful to offer a child some small reward each time the child goes to the bathroom in the toilet. As the child becomes proficient at potty-training, the reward is slowly stopped. Training helps a child form habits and develop proficiency, so rewards may be helpful on this level. Rewards may also be useful when you are trying to help your child break a bad habit. Habits are done unconsciously; for retraining, rewards could be a positive motivator.

However, beyond that, we must be very discerning and limited in how we reward our children. *Don't* pay children to behave well. For example, don't say, "If you sit still and be quiet, I will give you an ice cream cone." Proper behavior should just be expected. Don't use rewards as your primary parenting tool.

Remember: What is our goal as parents? We are training our children so they will be able to stand on their own feet and function as adults. We don't want children who will only do things if they "get" something in return, with the ante always going up.

We also don't want rewards to result in having the opposite effect and decrease our children's intrinsic motivation. Instead, we want our children to *want* to do well, think of others, feel good about their abilities, and take on challenges, knowing that it is learning through failure that brings about success. By thinking about how we reward our children and being intentional in providing opportunities so they feel intrinsic rewards, we can teach our children that our family is a team and we all need to work together for the good of the team. It may take some thought and creativity to develop this intrinsic motivation, but the long-term benefits are great.

As we do this, it is always important to remind our kids that we love them for who they are, not based on their performance. A scene from *The Andy Griffith Show* illustrates this well. In the episode, "Opie's Ill-Gotten Gain," Opie had been really struggling in school. When he came home with a report card full of straight As, his father went crazy with praise and rewards. Opie got a new bicycle and his father bragged to everyone about his son's grades and how smart he was. However, the next day in school, Opie's teacher told him that she had made a mistake on his report card, and gave him his correct one, which contained Cs, Ds, and an F. He wanted to explain the situation to his dad, but his dad was too busy praising him to listen. So Opie ran away. When Andy found Opie walking alongside a road, he stopped to talk with him. Opie explained the mix-up with his report card. He had wanted to tell him about it, but he worried about how disappointed his dad would be, so decided to run away until he could do something his dad would be proud of. His dad realized that he had put way too much emphasis on his good report card, but what was really important was that he loved his son and was proud of him for just being his son. He asked Opie to just do the best he could and he would love him no matter what.[61]

The reward system is deeply imbedded in our culture, and I realize there are people who may disagree with the content in this chapter. Yet I also know that many of you will be nodding your head in agreement. After I taught this topic in my parenting class, one couple was nodding their head and chuckling. Recently, they had promised to reward their daughter with a trip to a local ice cream stand if she kept her arms in the air while she was on the court during her basketball game. It worked: she did a great job keeping her arms up and active while playing in that game. Her parents were so proud at how well their reward had worked. This was short-lived, however. The game the following week was a disaster. Without the reward, her arms hung at her side, and she played much more poorly than she had prior to having the reward offered.

I want you to start thinking about how you can increase intrinsic motivation in your children rather than have them dependent on getting rewards and praise. We want to raise children who become adults who are self-motivated and follow their passions. As Kevin Leman reminds us, praise God, but *encourage* our children.

1. How do you use rewards in your family?
2. What results have you seen when you have used them?
3. What changes would you like to make?

4Cs

CHAPTER 10

Freedom Through Boundaries

PARENTING POINT: How we parent today is laying the foundation for who our children will be in 20 years.

At this point in the book, I think it's important to remember *why* we are doing this. We have covered a lot of ground, and some of it has been very difficult and will continue to be difficult as we attempt to put these lessons into practice. So remember: How we parent today is laying the foundation for who our children will be in 20 years. When they are young, your children will be parent-led and controlled out of necessity. But as they grow, our goal is that our children will become self-controlled. So even though it is difficult, it is important to be intentional now so our children will be prepared for life as they grow up. We don't want our children to be dependent on us in a childlike way when they are adults; instead, we want our children to be responsible, hard-working, kind, and independent, with defined goals and a promising future.

How can we accomplish this? In order to move to the parenting style we want—authoritative, which is high on both discipline and love—we must remember the key: establishing boundaries. What are your house rules, spoken and unspoken? It is so important to take the time to have them defined and taught. This is where implementing the 4 Cs becomes crucial. In order to do this properly, you must first decide your house rules and communicate them. Then you have to coach your child, teaching them what you expect prior to implementing consequences. Do not skip to consequences if you have not instructed and taught *first*. Once kids know and understand the boundaries, then those boundaries must be consistently enforced.

There is a cute children's book by Judy Delton called, *I'm Telling You Now,* in which a little boy constantly finds unknowingly mischievous things to do, like climbing the ladder and calling to his mom from the roof. His mother gasps, has him come down, and tells him he must never climb roofs, and he says, "You never told me." And his mother replies, "I am telling you now."[62]

The truth is, I think parents often think that kids know things that have never actually been taught. Homes should have rules and boundaries, but they must be clear, predictable, and—most importantly—taught.

Boundaries are a good thing; it might sound contradictory, but they actually give us freedom. For example, can you imagine driving across a long bridge that had no railings? The presence of those railings gives us the security we need to drive across that bridge. It is just this kind of feeling of security your child is after when he challenges you to set firm and consistent limits and boundaries for him. When you set solid limits and boundaries for your child, you are sending him a clear message that says, "I care about you, and I want you to be safe and feel secure as you learn about the world. I will always be here to love and guide you."

Some parents seem to have difficulty setting and enforcing limits and boundaries for their children; they would rather be their child's friend. Some may be insecure in their own lives and experiences and are inadequately prepared to provide a secure environment for their children. On the other end of the spectrum, there are parents who are overly controlling, have too many boundaries, or are abusive.

Balance is key; this means having boundaries and discipline that are fair and reasonable, but still allowing room for the child to learn, grow, and even make mistakes. The boundaries aren't meant to wall kids in; they should guide them toward the right path. Your child is looking to you to help them navigate life. Children need to know that you love them and will guide them, and an important part of guiding and discipline is teaching them and allowing them opportunities to grow, learn, and fail.

To help with creating house rules, we must first understand what makes a rule effective. A family rule is any demand or expectation by the parent on a child. A rule is *effective* if it is:

- **DEFINABLE**: It is very specific and clear.
- **REASONABLE**: It must be age-appropriate for a child to follow it.
- **ENFORCED**: We as parents must follow through and enforce the rule, or we don't make that rule at all.[63]

These characteristics are easy to define but often difficult to put into place. In our house, one of our rules is, "Our children must make their beds, or they won't get dessert." I taught them this rule; I even made signs and put them on my refrigerator and pantry. It is *definable* and *reasonable*, but where I have fallen short is not *enforcing* this rule. Therefore, this rule has been completely ineffective in my home. I want my kids to follow this rule. Making the bed is such a simple habit to do, and it helps keep our home tidy. I also find that when a bed is made, a child is more likely to put away their clothes and keep the rest of the room neater. According to a survey of 68,000 people by Hunch.com, 71 percent of bed-makers consider themselves happy, but only 38 percent of non-bed makers are happy. According to Gretchen Rubin, author of *The Happiness Project*, bed-making is a keystone habit, one that starts other good habits and is therefore, "the number one most impactful change people made."[64] If I want this rule to be followed, I need to start enforcing it. Once I start enforcing it, I know over time my children will wake up and make their beds. Who wouldn't want happier and more motivated children?

Each of our homes will have its own "vibe" and thus will have different boundaries; regardless, we all need to take an intentional look at our boundaries with a mentality of long-term thinking. What skills and character traits do we want our children to have as adults? Formulate a list of those, and then pick the top 10 you want to make sure your children learn. After making this list, write down a family rule that corresponds with each. This will give you a framework for your family's boundaries.

For example, one rule in our family is that we speak to others with respect. Learning to be respectful will help our kids in future relationships, jobs, and everyday life. Some of my kids have tested this boundary more than others, but I have found that it has been helpful to teach this at young ages, before they become disrespectful teenagers. This is something that we had to work on with my youngest. When he asked me to get something in a disrespectful way, I explained that I wouldn't get it for him if he asked in that way. I reminded him that speaking that way is unpleasant and disrespectful, and I then told him how to respectfully ask for something using the word "please." He then asked again using nicer words and tone. This only took a few weeks, and he spoke in a much more respectful way. If your child asks for something disrespectfully, don't grumble and get it anyway; wait until he asks in the correct way before fulfilling the request. This is all part of training. It takes time, but eventually kids learn how to be kind and polite, which will carry over into how they speak to others in their lives.

Because we are Christian and believe that it is great to talk to and about God, but it is wrong to say, "God" in anger or when not referring to God, so we have a family rule about that. There have been many times throughout the years when neighbors have come to play at our house and have not had this boundary in their own family. In this case, I explain our rule and what it means; I even validate that I understand this may be different from what they are used to, but ultimately, I remind them that in our house, it isn't allowed. Sometimes kids have stopped coming over for a period of time after these conversations, but eventually, those kids started coming over to play and learned to follow our house's rule when at our house. My teens have had these discussions with their friends themselves. As adults, we also need to follow the rules we establish in our homes, since they are *caught*, not taught. Kids are watching us and learning all the time.

Being honest is another rule in our home; this one is especially important for parents to model to their kids and to each other. Dave and I have worked hard to have complete transparency within our marriage—not through one of us forcing the other to do so (that can quickly escalate into abuse), but because we both mutually want to build trust and keep all doors open for conversation and honesty. For example, we don't have private passwords or separate checking accounts; Dave is welcome to see any of my correspondences, and I can see his. I have seen major problems in marriages when there are private emails or other correspondences, especially with today's easy access to so much and so many people on the internet. In our life, being transparent and honest in our marriage, in our friendships, and with our children has been beneficial in many ways.

When loading the car at Walmart a while ago, I noticed a small container of food coloring in the corner of my cart. I wasn't sure if it had rolled out of a bag, or if it had never gone through the check-out and thus wasn't paid for. It was snowing, and we were in a hurry, so I left and checked the receipt when I got home. Sure enough, I hadn't been charged for it. The next time I was in Walmart, I explained what had happened and paid for the coloring. Sophia was with me to see how I handled the situation. Our children are always watching us; what we do speaks louder than what we say.

I have found that some children have more trouble with lying than others. It makes me feel like a failure as a parent when my children lie, and it is a hard issue to fix. Yet I know that lying can destroy relationships and lives. Little children lie because they don't want to get in trouble, or they don't want to do something. Also, be aware that distinguishing between truth and lies can be confusing for young children. We read books and play pretend; they hear about Santa Claus and the Easter Bunny; so understanding the difference between fantasy and truth will have to be taught and learned. Interestingly, research by Victoria Talwar found that children who were afraid of punishment were *less* likely to tell the truth.[65] Be careful to avoid relational consequences like guilt, shame, condemnation, or abandonment. We want to create an environment for our children where we can teach that speaking truthfully is not only the right thing to do, it makes them feel better.

Being responsible is another rule in our home. Responsibility includes taking ownership and being accountable for your actions. It also includes being reliable, dependable, and hard-working. Taking responsibility for our own feelings, attitudes, behaviors, choices, thoughts, and actions is so important. My attitude is *my* problem. The avoidance of taking responsibility goes all the way back to the first humans, Adam and Eve, when Eve blamed the serpent and Adam blamed Eve after eating the forbidden fruit. However, we are all accountable to God for our lives. (II Corinthians 5:10)

When something happens in your family, is there always a blame game? Is it always someone else's fault? Do we have children who do this? Do *we* do this? Do we blame the traffic, red light, or slow cars in front of us, or do we accept responsibility for not leaving early enough? Do we work hard and get things done, or do we just sit around blaming everyone else for not doing enough? Do we expect our children to do their share and help, or do we do it for them? Yes, bad things do happen in which we have no fault, but many times, we do have something to do with the situation. Learning to accept responsibility will set children up for success.

Our children are going to be exposed to various expectations at school, activities, church, and friends' homes. As we teach our family's boundaries, you can talk about boundaries in other places. There will be times when they go to a friend's house and they may need to take their shoes off when they enter the home or the food served is totally different. Just as we would like others to be sensitive to boundaries in our home, we can also teach our children to be sensitive to boundaries that might be different from their own. I do want my children to be kind and respectful to others, just as I would like others to be respectful to them.

Learning by Reading Stories Aloud

One great way to teach boundaries and life issues is through reading to your children. The benefits are priceless. The Program for International Student Assessment (PISA) is a fascinating international study done every three years by the Organization for Economic Cooperation and Development (OECD). The study not only looks at test scores, but also interviews 5,000 of their parents to look at their parenting styles, and what it has revealed about reading to children is important. Those children whose parents read to them regularly during their first year of primary school have significantly higher PISA scores at 15 years old, regardless of socioeconomic background. The PISA study also looks at how children are able to solve real-life situations, and those children whose parents read to them regularly scored much higher on this matter. Additionally, the number of books in their home also affected students' reading performance. The students with 100 books at home scored one grade higher and students with 500 or more books at home scored two grades higher than those with few or no books at home.[66]

Quality literature is filled with real-life struggles and situations children and adults can relate to and talk about. Books open doors to discussions and strengthen relationships. When your child sees a character in a book struggling with lying, your child can see the hole being dug, can perhaps relate to the character's feelings of guilt, and can witness and understand the consequences. It is a perfect segue into a conversation about good and bad choices with your kids.

In our family, we have also found that books provide a unique "common language." I can't believe how often life triggers quotes from our favorite books. No matter the age of your children, find good quality literature. I never tire from reading high-quality literature to my kids, and I stay away from books based on children's TV shows. If you cannot afford to buy books, make regular visits to your library. If it is a small library, see if they do a library lending program with other libraries so that you can get more books. Visit my website at www.parentingsensibly. com for book recommendations.

In order to create a solid, secure base from which your child can learn and grow into a responsible adult with good character and healthy boundaries, you need to lay a solid foundation today. Take the time to create a list of rules/boundaries with consequences and use them to teach and guide your children.

1. Write down your family's most important boundaries/rules.
2. Make sure they are defined, reasonable, and enforceable.
3. Have a family meeting to discuss them; make it fun and light.
4. Start a bedtime reading habit, even with school-aged children.

SECTION 3

Preparing Our Children for Success in Adulthood

As we talk about parenting, we have to ask the question: What *really* makes an impact in our children's growth into adulthood?

Dan Kindlon, author of *Too Much of a Good Thing: Raising Children of Character in an Indulgent Age*,[67] did a study in 2000 to identify risk factors for teenage problems like substance abuse, eating disorders, depression, and anxiety—common enough topics to study, but he also looked at parenting styles and the teens' character traits, like being self-centered, spoiled, or lazy. He gave questionnaires to 650 upper-middle-class and wealthy teenagers from all over the U.S. He also surveyed over 1,000 parents—some parents of teenagers, some with young children. Among his fascinating findings:

- Though 40 percent of teenagers said they were seriously depressed, very few parents said their teens were depressed.
- Sixty percent of teens had used tobacco, alcohol, or other illegal drugs in the previous month.
- Sixty percent of parents said they spoiled their children (many of the kids agreed).
- Nearly half of the parents said they were less strict than their parents.

There is a popular parenting myth: If I just give my kids what they want, it will make them happy, and they will be fine as they grow older. But the reality is that spoiling them isn't going to be helpful for their future well-being. Kindlon found that giving kids excess material things and being less strict are actually risk factors for drug use. Not eating together as a family is a risk factor for both drug use and depression. Giving allowance without requiring any chores is a risk factor for depression and—not surprisingly—for self-centeredness.

On the positive side, 12 percent of the teenagers interviewed in the study were doing well. They didn't use drugs; they weren't mean, lazy, self-centered, spoiled, anxious, or depressed; they didn't think it was okay for 13-year-olds to have oral sex. Interestingly, this 12 percent had five things in common:

1. Their families frequently ate dinner together.
2. They regularly did community service.
3. They had to keep their rooms clean.
4. Their parents weren't divorced.
5. They weren't allowed to have a phone in their room. (Note that this study was done in 2000.)

Although this study was done a while ago, I find it fascinating. If you asked 100 parents what things make the most difference for the long-term well-being of their kids, what would they list? Do they prioritize their time, energy, and money on sports, clubs, tutors and the like, or do they focus on one or two of the things listed above?

One of most surprising aspects of Kindlon's study revealed that it wasn't material things or activities that played a major role in a child's avoidance of drugs, alcohol, sex, depression, and anxiety. Instead it was having responsibilities, eating dinner together, and doing community service. These are all things we can incorporate into our parenting. The last two factors—having parents who weren't divorced and not having a phone in the bedroom—are harder to control. Smart phones are now with many teens at all times.

This is why, in this last section of the book, I will focus on the first three factors that we can do something about: family dinners, community service, and chores. Additionally, I will discuss a number of other critical topics that need to be addressed as our children grow older. Each of these is an area in which children will need training and guidance if they are to be able to soar independently and successfully someday. Does this mean that by doing these things, we will guarantee our children will be free from emotional struggles or issues with addiction? No—unfortunately, nothing we do can guarantee that. However, teaching and training in these areas throughout our children's growing-up years is a wise investment—one that I believe will have life-long returns.

CHAPTER 11

Family Dinners: Will You Come Eat With Us?

 PARENTING POINT: Families who eat together, stay together.

"**M**om, what's for dinner?"

This was the question I dreaded. It made me feel like an inadequate mom. When my kids were younger, our meal repertoire was painfully small, and we were all sick of eating the same things: pizza, grilled cheese, ham steaks and hash brown casserole, chicken strips, pancakes, French toast, spaghetti, and a few more things. I'd go grocery shopping, come home, and still have no idea what to fix. The meat I bought would be quickly frozen so it would not go bad, and then I didn't know what to do with the large solid block of meat. Often, it would sit in the freezer for so long I would eventually throw it away.

Why, I wondered, was cooking so important for families to master? What's the big deal about family dinners, anyway?

It turns out that kids who eat family dinners together have a lower incidence of drug and alcohol use and do better academically. As we highlighted in the introduction to this unit, Dan Kindlon's study[68] found that eating family dinners together is one of five things teens who are doing well have in common.

Additionally,

> "The National Center on Addiction and Substance Abuse has surveyed thousands of American teens and their parents to identify situations and circumstances that influence the risk of teen substance abuse. What we have learned is that parental engagement in children's lives is fundamental to keeping children away from tobacco, alcohol and other drugs, and that parents have the greatest influence on whether their teens will choose not to use substances. Our surveys have consistently found a relationship between children having frequent dinners with their parents and a decreased risk of their smoking, drinking or using other drugs, and that parental engagement fostered around the dinner table is one of the most potent tools to help parents raise healthy, drug-free children. Simply put: frequent family dinners make a big difference."[69]

Academic success is another benefit from eating frequent family meals. Dr. Catherine Snow, at the Graduate School of Education at Harvard, found that young children who had regular family meals had larger vocabularies and better reading skills.[70] There was also a positive correlation between high achievement test scores for students ages 7-11, and eating frequent family meals, according to a study at the University of Illinois.[71] Not only with younger kids, but family meals were also a strong predictor of academic success for high school students.[72] [73]

Home-cooked meals are often healthier for our kids (and for us). On any given day, a third of children in the United States eat fast food, which contains more sugar, fat, salt, and calories than most food prepared at home.[74] French fries are the most frequently eaten "vegetable" in America.[75] In 2012, companies spent $4.6 billion to advertise mainly unhealthy food to children and teens. Did you know that McDonald's is the largest toy distributor in the world? Quebec saw a problem with targeting children and banned advertising of fast foods to children about 30 years ago. As a result, 38 percent fewer children in Quebec eat fast food than in the neighboring province of Ontario. Unfortunately, the U.S. does not have the same restrictions.[76] However, students who ate more family meals consumed fewer soft drinks; ate more fruits and vegetables, grains, and calcium-rich food; had fewer concerns about body weight; and made healthier eating choices. There was also a reduction in extreme weight control behavior/disordered eating among adolescent girls who had frequent family meals.[77]

Although home-cooked meals are usually healthier, that's not the most important reason to eat together around the dinner table; time to connect and engage as a family is. This time for connection reduces stress and tensions and enhances emotional well-being. In one study, when teens experienced a serious problem, those who ate with their family more than five days per week were more likely to go to their parents for advice.[78] Interestingly, 79 percent of teens not only enjoyed dinner with their families, but preferred that to watching TV and rated the enjoyment as high as going on vacation![79] Eating family meals while watching TV or other distractions has negative effects. This means we *must leave technology away from the table!* In today's technology-driven society, this is difficult, but it is so important to our parenting. Eat together at the table; don't have a TV, laptops, phones, iPads, or other devices at the table. Instead, use that time to dialog with your children. Ask what their favorite part of the day was. What was the hardest? Show an interest in your kids. Be present.

To help us have active discussion at the dinner table, we always keep a copy of the book, *Dinner Talk: 365 Engaging Conversation Starters to Help You and Your Family Connect*, nearby. Someone picks a question, and we go around the table answering it. We have done this for so long that often we now make up our own questions. Use meal times to establish a relationship with your kids; that time is not just about the food.

What if I Don't Know How to Cook?

I was pretty good at baking because I did a lot of it growing up. Baking was something I enjoyed, and it was rewarding to see my treats quickly devoured by my brothers and—when I was older—my husband and children.

My cooking skills, however, were not as good. Growing up, I did help my mom with some cooking, but she had to do very quick dinners because of her work schedule. She taught music lessons in our home, so she usually worked from the time school got out each day until at least 6:30 p.m. It was the late 1970s and early 1980s; we were happy that the microwave had been invented! Much of our food was fried or microwaved. Suffice it to say, I didn't have a lot of diverse cooking skills when I was married. The kids always joked, "Mom is a good baker, but not a very good cook."

However, as our kids grew older and became involved in more activities, preparing food and eating together at home became a big challenge for our family. It was about this time that I first went to a meal prep business; they had the recipes and ingredients all laid out, and customers like me would go from station to station filling a Ziploc bag or 9x13 aluminum pan with the ingredients. It took trying a few venues before I found one I liked, but it worked out very well for our family. My kids tried new foods, and I learned to cook, one recipe at a time. Better yet, I had food that could be cooked in a crockpot or was ready to bake as soon as we got home from swim practice or whatever other activities took us out of the house for the day. I no longer dreaded the infamous question of "What's for dinner, Mom?"

We relied on that meal prep business until we moved across the country from Seattle to Delaware; at that point, we had five sons, a 15-month-old daughter, and I was 30 weeks pregnant with identical twins. Two weeks after that move, the twins were born by emergency C-section and spent their first month in the NICU; I spent a lot of time traveling to and from the hospital to be with them.

We were in a new state, settling into a new house, with new babies in the family, and no friends or family nearby; I *had* to figure out some method of feeding my growing family. So I took all I had learned at the meal prep business and started to figure out how to do monthly freezer meals myself.

This has revolutionized our dinner time. Best of all, I don't have to think about dinner; I just have to remember to take it out of the freezer a day or two ahead of time and cook it. This takes the stress out of preparing meals on a daily basis. This method of meal planning does take focused time and effort for two-to-three days every five weeks, but it frees up time making dinner during those five weeks.

If you love to cook daily and that is working for you, keep it up—that is awesome! If you have a cooking routine that works for your family and encourages everyone to sit together and engage with each other at the dinner table, then don't feel any need to change it. The method my family and I use is only one way; remember, there are many ways to put a home-cooked meal on your family's table. What's most important is that your family is eating together.

Get Your Kids Involved With Cooking!

In my experience, kids are much more excited about eating as a family if they help choose meals, and they are much more likely to eat new things if they help prepare them. Getting the kids involved in meal planning will also teach them an important life skill. Use the time you spend preparing a meal as a learning opportunity—and expect that they won't always get it right. It is through their mistakes that they will learn—and, speaking from experience, you'll get some funny family stories out of it!

Over the years, my kids have put in one *cup* of chopped garlic instead of one *tablespoon*. We just rinsed off the meat and started again. Recently, Sophia has been wanting to make cupcakes. Twice, she picked out a recipe online and made them; both times ended up with batches of inedible cupcakes. In the course of making a third recipe, she realized that the last time she tried baking cupcakes she used a *tablespoon* instead of a *teaspoon* of baking soda, which resulted in the cupcakes bubbling out of the cupcake pan. It was a great lesson learned, and the latest batch of cupcakes was wonderful. However, she was puzzled by the frosting. When I tasted it, it was obvious that she had used regular sugar, not powdered sugar, so the frosting was granular. Another lesson learned for the future!

Allow your children to make the mistakes, because the lesson learned will have a much greater impact than if you hover and micromanage their every move or, worse yet, not allow them the opportunity to try.

Setting an Example

Remember that good habits are caught, not taught. This is just as true when it comes to our food choices and making sure they're healthy. Your kids will imitate your eating patterns and habits. Kids need you to set a good example and guide them. They do not have a natural instinct for healthy eating choices. The food in your house is food that you have purchased. It is up to you to fill your refrigerator and cupboards with healthy food choices. For me, I have little self-control if potato chips are in the house. My kids have other temptations. It is much better for all of us if I buy those foods very infrequently, just on special occasions.

I find that my kids snack on fruit when it is out and accessible. We frequently have apples and peanut butter, and it is great to have whatever fruit is in season wherever we are living. Because we've been able to live in houses with a decent amount of land, we've also been able to grow different fruits and vegetables for our family to use. In Washington state, we had an abundance of blackberries; in Delaware, it was raspberries. In our current house in Maryland, we are still working towards getting our raspberries, blackberries, and apples established, but our strawberries and tomatoes have been wonderful. It is a goal for me to have that, because I love having my kids snack from the garden while playing outside.

As you shop for food for your family, a good thing to keep in mind is that the darker the color of a vegetable, the higher its nutritional value. Teach balanced nutrition and moderation. I think that, broadly speaking for those of us living in the U.S., reducing our sugar consumption is a good goal. When I made it a point to start reading food labels, I realized that added sugar is in everything from ketchup to peanut butter to marinara sauce. If you look at the labels, you can find great tasting products without the added sugar. Additionally, make sure you offer proper proportions for the child's size and age; don't give them adult portions and then make them clean their plate if they can't finish it.

Also, remember that children don't have the same palate as adults. What did *you* eat when you were a child? Did your tastes change and develop with age? It can take up to 20 exposures to a food for someone to develop a liking for it. Your child may not like something the first 19 times, but on that 20th time, she may realize she does in fact like it. I have seen the whole gamut with my kids. I have had children as young as one year old like salsa, coleslaw, and lemons. I have children who eat just about everything, and others who only eat a small number of things. You will need to decide how to handle this, whether it is by making the child try a bite of everything on their plate, or perhaps by having the child make himself something else if he chooses not to eat what is for dinner. I do not recommend being a short-order cook to make something different for each child (unless there is a need to because of food allergies or other health concerns). However, recognize that it can take time for children to develop a taste for different foods.

Keep the Goal in Mind

I will be the first to admit that prioritizing home-cooked meals with your family is more work, but not necessarily more time. You may spend a lot of time on a meal that the rest of your family ends up not liking (and they won't be afraid to let you know just how much they don't like it). You will have food that is overcooked, undercooked, and just plain *wrong*. You'll have to work to get everyone's schedules lined up so you can actually sit down to enjoy the food together. And even when everything goes right, you'll still have some dishes to clean up at the end of the day!

On days when I'm faced with doing a lot of meal prep cooking that I don't necessarily want to do, or it seems really difficult to try and get all members of our family to sit down together for a meal because of conflicting schedules, I think about holiday dinners. I think one of the things we all love the most about holidays like Christmas, Thanksgiving, and Easter is the act of gathering around the table for good food and fellowship. We aren't rushing off to do something else or go somewhere; we are there to feast and enjoy one another's company.

Should those few days a year be the only time we do this? I don't think so—and, more importantly, the research tells us it shouldn't be that way![80] We have to start setting dinner as a priority and focusing on changes we need to make to put the family meal table back into our lives. Remember: "Families who eat together, stay together." Let's make dinner together—at home—a priority and an intentional time to connect with our children.

1. What do your current meal times look like?
2. What could you do to increase the number of dinners you eat together as a family?
3. How could you involve your children in making dinners?

CHAPTER 12

Serving Others: The Antidote for Self-Centeredness

PARENTING POINT: It is more blessed to give than to receive. (Acts 20:35 NIV)[81]

"My little Veruca got more and more upset each day, and every time I went home she would scream at me, '*Where's my Golden Ticket! I want my Golden Ticket!*' And she would lie for hours on the floor, kicking and yelling in the most disturbing way. Well, sir, I just hated to see my little girl feeling unhappy like that, so I vowed I would keep up the search until I'd got her what she wanted."

   Mr. Salt from Roald Dahl, *Charlie and the Chocolate Factory*[82]

Humorous as it is, this father's darling Veruca is easily identified as the self-serving kid whose spoiled childhood represents how badly things can go when parents emphasize serving their kids over helping them to serve others. Serving others takes our eyes off ourselves, something that is so necessary in this age of entitlement.

We'll look at the best ways to get your kids focused on serving others and the joy that it can bring to their lives. First, let's look at entitlement and how to overcome this common barrier to serving others.

What is Entitlement?

When we feel entitled to something, we believe that it should come to us without effort; in other words, we deserve something for no apparent reason. A sense of entitlement has likely been a consistent character trait among young people for generations; consider the remark, "kids these days." So this selfishness is not new, but its present incarnation may be a function of changing technology and how we communicate. In my own lifetime, U.S. society has become more automated, more digitalized, and glutted with things to buy, certainly affecting kids' greed. There are signs of entitlement among children and adults that cause issues in elementary, high school, and college classrooms, as well as in the workplace. Entitlement can cause a decrease in work ethic, a lack of focus, and problems with one's use of technology. As we train our children in areas of self-motivation, respect, responsibility, and appropriate behavior and presentation, our teaching will carry over to the workplace, where the stakes are higher, so it's critical that these lessons are learned early.

Here's the main problem with behaviors that arise out of an entitlement mentality: they're learned—and even encouraged—by adults. For example, my neighbor was a coach for her 8-year-old daughter's softball team. At the first game, the coaches were told that each girl would get up to seven pitches to hit the ball. My neighbor was appalled; she reminded the others that the rules of the game are three strikes for an out. She pointed out that kids need to learn that it's okay to strike out; it's part of the learning process, and they will learn to get better over time. The game was played with those rules. Afterward, the other coach told her that it was a great lesson for the kids, and it was the first game he'd attended for this age group where all the innings had been completed. We need to be aware of the messages we are sending our kids and how they may affect them; do we want to increase the probability that a young softball player will make it to first base, or do we want to play the game as it was designed, knowing the players may feel greater disappointment but ultimately learn the valuable lesson of coping with failure and working hard to overcome defeat? Children need our guidance and to observe our actions as well. Make sure our work ethic, our diligence, the respect we demonstrate for others, and the accountability we take is what we want them to establish as they form their own pathway through the formative years.

Fixing the Problem

What does all this talk about entitlement have to do with raising kids, and why would that make a difference in a kid's life? We are by nature self-centered, but that isn't a healthy way to be. There is truth to the statement, "It is more blessed to give than to receive." Serving others forces us to shift our attention from our own (typically selfish) wants and needs and instead gives us a different perspective. This is exactly what our children need to learn and experience as well. You may be thinking, "But is it really that important?" Considering that serving others is one of the five common factors in the lives of teenagers who are not depressed, anxious, using drugs or alcohol, or have lax attitudes about sex, I would say, "Yes!"[83]

Serving others is a key to increasing our own happiness, our emotional and physical well-being, and our levels of gratitude. Teenagers who volunteer have higher grades and self-esteem, and lower drug use, teen pregnancy rates, and drop-out rates than those who do not serve in a volunteer capacity. Interestingly, even children who are forced to volunteer fare better than kids who don't volunteer at all.[84]

Giving children an opportunity to serve opens their eyes to the reality that the majority of people don't have everything they do, and it helps them begin to consider why this is so. Especially for kids from middle- and upper-middle-class families, it creates a sense of gratitude for what they do have and cultivates compassion and the desire to give to others. It also encourages them to develop relationships with people who come from vastly disparate backgrounds, broadening their understanding of the world around them and encouraging them to engage with viewpoints that are different than their own.

Serving in the Community

There are so many opportunities that you can provide for your children to serve. Last year, our kids assembled baggies filled with a water bottle, some snack foods, and basic necessities during our church's children's ministry program. Armed with something to give, my kids were on the lookout for homeless people when we were driving. Instead of ignoring those who are so often overlooked in our society, my kids actively sought to engage with them, and the joy they felt in giving the bags and offering even that smallest bit of help made them want to give more. Activities like this also give us an opportunity to talk about homelessness and some of its underlying causes, as well as what we can do to make a difference.

Preparing food is a tremendous way to serve others. When you are baking some cookies, for example, make a few extras and bring them over to an elderly neighbor or someone who is having a rough time. By involving your children in this activity, you're not only teaching them an important skill in the kitchen, but you're also showing them a simple but powerful way to give to and serve others. My oldest son, Josh, has been baking cookies to give away for years; he finds great joy in being able to provide a friend, a family member, or even a complete stranger a home-baked sweet treat. I think the simple gift of freshly baked goods has been lost in our current generation, but it can do wonders for lifting the spirits of someone who is depressed, lonely, sick, or overwhelmed.

It's also powerful to be on the receiving end of this care. I learned this after I broke my foot while 30 weeks pregnant with Asher, my tenth child. Not only were we blessed by food, but a friend came over for a few hours to help me clean my house when I was stressed about how out-of-hand things were getting with me out of commission. It was a tremendous relief and blessing to have this kind of care shown to me and my family, and so being able to serve others in this way is even more meaningful to me now.

Another fairly simple act of service you can do is have your child go through their clothes and toys a couple times a year and give away those things that no longer fit or items they don't wear or play with. This may be difficult sometimes as you pass down clothes and toys to younger siblings (we do this a lot), but it is still a good practice; there may be more to get rid of than you think. Throw away broken things and worn-out clothes, but bless others with things your kids no longer use or items that are duplicates. It's understandable that parents want to buy their children material things, but if kids only experience "getting," they become self-centered. Developing a pattern of giving from a young age will benefit them greatly. They will become less attached to material things and more prone to giving when they see a need.

Serving others doesn't have to be a planned event; ideally, it will become your natural way to do life. As your children get older, they will be able to use the talents and skills they are developing to serve in other unique ways. As my boys have aged, they have worked alongside my husband on several home-repair projects for people in need. They've also served on local and foreign mission projects through our church and have applied previous knowledge and also learned new skills, such as replacing roofs, mixing and pouring concrete, and helping with kids' programs. When they see the tough situations people live in and have the opportunity to serve, they not only feel the joy of giving, but they also cultivate greater gratitude for what they have.

Living life this way also encourages you to interact with those with whom, for whatever reason, you may not have interacted or built relationships with before. When I was growing up, my mom was the choir director and organist at our church. She had a heart for people in nursing homes, so a couple times a year, we would head out to the local nursing homes to sing. One place we always went was the county health care center, where severely disabled adults were cared for. When we were singing our songs, they would be so overjoyed that they would clap and cry out. We would finish our songs and mingle and talk to everyone. There were certainly awkward moments, but the experience made me much more comfortable around people with special needs. Because our church hosts an annual community event for the local special needs community, my children have had the privilege to help with the jumping castles for the past three years. Like with many serving opportunities that have become expected, natural parts of our life together, my kids just view it as a fun thing to do.

Putting Our Money Where Our Service Is

Time is a valuable resource, and serving firsthand gives you and your family unique connections and experiences with others. But we should not overlook the importance of giving financially for the benefit of others. Our monetary donations should be just as intentional and meaningful as our gifts of time.

Our family donates to a number of different organizations. We are particular fans of the organization Kiva,[85] which allows you to give microfinancing loans in $25 increments to people all over the world. You will get your money back as the person repays the loan, and then you can re-invest that money into a loan for someone else. We like Kiva because it gives our children the opportunity to see the variety of businesses that are started around the world, and it also shows them the power of these small loans for improving others' lives. We have our kids help pick out the people to whom we loan money, and together we learn where they live and how the loan will help them.

Sponsoring a child through organizations like Compassion International[86] allows for a kid-to-kid service connection. These organizations provide food, clothing, education, and other needs for under-resourced children and their communities, and Compassion also encourages you and your family to write letters and develop a relationship with the child you sponsor. Your children can draw pictures or write letters to that child.

We currently support two children: one in Columbia and one in Ethiopia. We sponsored a boy in Indonesia for several years until his family moved away from his Compassion center. One letter we got from him explained the kind of house he lived in and said that his light source was "light bottles." We were able to look up light bottles and watch a video about them. They are two-liter plastic bottles filled with water and put through a roof. During the day, they help disperse light in the house quite effectively, about equivalent to a 60-watt light bulb. Little moments like this provide unique lessons and points of connection with people from a variety of cultures around the world.

In addition to "organized" giving like these opportunities, practice random act of kindness. I challenge you to try giving a large tip to someone—a waiter, waitress, or even someone on the street—and see the impact it has for you. Sophia once begged to go with Dave to get some food at a Japanese take-out restaurant. After Dave paid, Sophia quietly slipped $20 of her own money into the tip jar, which was a month's worth of earnings for her. She did it totally anonymously and left. The satisfaction of supporting people without something to gain is a joyous thing that we can all experience regardless of age or how much we give.

Whether it is through giving our money or our time, our example of generosity will make a far greater impact on our children than anything we encourage them to do through our words. Don't wait until you have all the time and money you think you need—if you do, you will never have enough of either. Just keep your eye out for needs around you. As you do, you'll find that you and your family will develop a sense of gratitude and a heart for others that you would never have had otherwise—and both of these will make your home a better place.

Serving at Home

It is fantastic to provide opportunities to serve others in the community, but developing that servant's heart within our homes is equally impactful. Yet oftentimes the home is the one place where practicing service is most difficult. If only I had a dollar for each time someone in my home said, "It's not mine" or "I didn't do it!" And how many times have we discussed the fact that it doesn't matter who did it, that we all need to pitch in and help? This is a tough topic, but overcoming this "me" viewpoint and morphing into "us" will transform your home and set your children up for future success in relationships, work, and marriage.

A couple months ago we got a new rescue puppy. The last thing I needed in my life was the work of a puppy, but my kids came to me with a proposal: "We all chipped in, so we have enough money to pay for the puppy. We will do all the training, clean-up, and cares. Could we please buy the puppy?" I reminded them about all the work a new puppy is, but they all agreed that they would do everything. They quickly wrote up a list of everyone's responsibilities, and we arranged to get the puppy. I would not have done this if my kids had not established accountability with responsibility in other areas already, because a pet is a long-term commitment.

Having a puppy again has been a lot of work for them. The responsibility has encouraged them to work together and do things that weren't always "their" pet chore, just for the sake of taking care of the dog and the commitment they took on when they bought the puppy. It is giving them great practice at responsibility; learning that while playing with the puppy is fun, it comes with a lot of work. It also has been a great lesson in serving together.

Not only with puppy cares, but in other areas as well, it is important to encourage that servant's heart within your family and household. Having a large family, it has been a natural process for my kids to help younger siblings, tie shoes, pour a drink, get strapped in a car seat, get ice and a Band-Aid when someone gets hurt. But no matter what size your family is, mutual care is so important to cultivate. Just as we serve our kids, it is equally critical that they learn to serve others with a good attitude and happy heart.

Giving When Time is Tight

We all lead busy lives. Many days, it seems like all we can do is scrape by in managing to keep all the balls in the air. I am *very* familiar with this; the days seem long and the nights short, and it feels like we can't possibly put one more thing in our schedule. However, I want to challenge you to make time for your family to serve others. It is time to open our eyes to those in need right in our back yard and commit to doing *something*. It can be as simple as the opportunity we recently had in Washington, D.C.. As soon as we found a bench to eat our picnic lunch, my daughter said, "Mom, we need to give that homeless man some water." We did, along with sharing the lunch we had brought. We want compassionate, kind, and grateful children, not self-absorbed, entitled children. Set an example by serving others, and, even more importantly, serving others *with* your children. Our family has found that when we serve through giving our time and money—even when we don't think we can afford either one—it still works out. The benefits we have gained as a family are immeasurable.

1. Have you had opportunities to serve with your children?
2. Brainstorm ways you could provide more opportunities to serve with them.
3. Depending on the age of your children, start teaching about needs you see around you: explain about homelessness, foodbanks, or how you could do something nice for an aging neighbor.

CHAPTER 13

Chores: Responsibilities Teach Responsibility

 PARENTING POINT: Don't do for your kids what they can do for themselves.

One of the hardest facts we must accept as parents is that our children's life skills are learned by doing, failing, and then mastering—not by watching or avoiding. No matter how much we want to protect our children from failure and pain, or do things for them when they are struggling, we must trust that they will learn best through their own personal experiences.

Swimming provides a great example of the value of learning from experience. According to the Centers for Disease Control and Prevention, 3,536 people die in the U.S. every year from non-boating, accidental drownings.[87] That amounts to roughly 10 deaths every day. Though sometimes factors like injuries or other circumstances may have an impact on a person's chance of survival, there is one best way to prevent drowning: Learn to swim. We can try to be diligent in watching children when they are near water; we can tell them the dangers of water; we can even explain the mechanics of swimming and what to do in an emergency. However, this will not be sufficient all—or even most—of the time. The skill simply has to be learned.

I have spent more than two decades watching kids learn to swim and am currently watching my youngest do so. One of the most important skills kids learn in swim lessons is what to do when they find themselves in water, even with their clothes on: They have to figure out how to float, get to the side, and pull themselves out of the water. Kids have to develop the strength it takes to hoist themselves out of the pool. They practice and practice, repeatedly jumping in, rolling to their back, turning themselves around, kicking to the side, reaching for the edge, and hoisting themselves out. Being able to survive in larger bodies of water will take years of practice, but these are important first steps in that process.

It is hard as a parent to watch children struggle in this setting; they get water in their eyes, swallow water, get cold, and generally do things they don't want to do. It is especially difficult when kids are afraid of the water. Some of my kids took to water very quickly and easily; others were scared and didn't want to go past their comfort zone. When my youngest was 3, he wanted nothing to do with lessons; putting his head underwater terrified him. But he continued with his lessons, and now, two years later, he has found the joy of water and is making great progress with his swimming skills. It was precisely by continuing to face his fears (in a setting where he was always completely safe) and working through those challenging aspects of learning to swim that he was able to conquer his fear and begin the journey to master his swimming skills.

This is true not just for swimming. Our children will need to learn many other skills to survive as independent adults, and they will need to practice—*a lot*—in order to be proficient and confident when life's hurdles come their way. Protecting them or doing things for them will never teach them the skills they need. They must learn by *doing*. This is why—as hard as it is—we must step back and allow our children to have opportunities to practice skills, feel uncomfortable, and fail so that they can learn what they need to know as they grow into adults.

Up until just a few generations ago in the U.S., children learned a lot of these kinds of skills and responsibilities by working alongside their parents as they grew up, taking on more and more responsibility around the house as they aged. Girls assisted their mothers with cooking, gardening, sewing, cleaning, and childcare, while boys worked alongside their dads on the farm, at the family store, or whatever their dad's trade was. My great-grandfather, for example, was a brick-layer, and several of his boys went on to own their own construction businesses.

I am *not* saying things were better then; nor do I think we need to go back to that way of life. But there *is* something we can learn from this lifestyle: The children were learning the responsibility, work ethic, and skills they needed so that by the time they were teens, they could step into the adults' roles.

Things are much different today. Kids spend more time in school and often don't work alongside their parents. They also spend a lot of time doing clubs, sports, and extracurricular activities. Their packed schedules leave far less time for working on basic life skills, and in the United States, most education programs are not designed for teaching those skills. This is why we as parents must provide opportunities for our children to learn responsibility and proficiency through chores. When it comes to practical life skills, chores are the best way to enable kids to have this kind of growth.

What's so Important About Chores?

Chores get a bad rap; even the word itself causes groaning and complaining. Yet research shows they are vitally important to our children's success. Remember that in Dan Kindlon's study, first mentioned in the Introduction to this section, it was one of the five factors that kids who were doing well had in common: Everyone had at least one chore. The children who were succeeding were not the ones who were just in sports or pursuing some other activity; nor were the children who were given more allowance or material things. Instead, it was the kids who had to do chores.[88]

Another 20-year longitudinal study showed similar conclusions. Marty Rossmann, emeritus associate professor of family education at the University of Minnesota, analyzed unexplored data in 2002 that had previously been collected on parenting styles from 1967-1987.[89] The data had been collected when the children in the study were aged 3-4 years, 9-10 years, 15-16 years, and one last time when they were in their 20s. Interestingly, the best predictor of study participants' success in their 20s was that they participated in household tasks at the age of 3-4. The kids who began doing chores at that age were learning responsibility, contributing to the family, and learning empathy and self-care. Additionally, the study showed that kids who didn't start chores until they were 9-10 years old did not do as well, and those who didn't start doing chores until they were teenagers did the worst; by then, they were too self-centered.

In other words, if a child starts doing chores when he's 3 or 4 he is more likely to be successful in his 20s. Children with chores will also be less likely to do drugs; drink alcohol; have eating disorders, anxiety, or depression; or have careless views about sex. It's true: Chores are *that* important!

The consequences of failing to use chores to do this kind of training can be immense. When our family moved to Arizona 25 years ago, we bought our first house from a man who owned several mattress stores. His wife had never liked the house, which her husband had picked out, so they bought a much bigger and more expensive one instead. When we took possession and were trying to move in, his family still hadn't moved completely out. Many of his employees were frantically throwing things into boxes and hauling them outside, but his teenage sons stood around and did nothing.

This house was priced low, even though it was only two years old, because the family—especially the teenagers—had trashed it. There were cigarette burns all over the carpet; closet doors were not on the hinges;

the screens were broken or hanging out of their frames because the teens would sit on the windowsill to smoke. Out in the tiny yard, Dave filled two—two!—five-gallon buckets full of doggie doo.

About six years later, we went to a furniture store to look at bunk beds, and the salesman said, "Do you remember me?" It was the former owner of our home. In the years since he sold us that house, his wife had died from lung cancer and had never been able enjoy their new house. In the midst of dealing with that tragedy, the man had given his successful, multi-site business to his two teenage sons—the ones who had done nothing to care for the house or help with the move and were in fact high school dropouts. They went on a spending spree for themselves and never ran the business with any sense; the business had gone bankrupt. Since that point, the salesman had remarried, had started having children again, and was trying to rebuild his life. He acknowledged how stupid he had been to expect his sons to take responsibility for a business when they had not done so in anything before and had never been trained or taught properly.

This is obviously an extreme example, but it's a poignant one. We really *must* begin preparing our kids for adulthood while they are still young. It will be much easier for them to learn responsibility with smaller things as young children than if we suddenly hand them large responsibilities when they're older.

Don't Do for Your Kids What They Can Do for Themselves

When we think about implementing chores in our families, it's common to think things like:

- It is easier for me to do it.
- My kids won't do it how I want it done.
- I have a housekeeper.
- I like to do it.

- I don't want the battle and whining.
- I will assign chores when they get older.

If we keep making these excuses, the years will go by, our kids will grow up, and soon it will be too late to teach them these responsibilities. Start today so that someday you can say, "I am so glad I did," instead of "I wish I had."

There has been a lot of discussion and research about how (and why) more and more adult children are living with their parents. According to Pew Research, about a third of 18-to-34-year-olds were living with their parents in 2016.[90] Now, there *are* situations that make this the best option for both parents and children, such as family illnesses, unexpected job loss, or financial difficulty for the children or the parents. Some families are also wanting to help a child save money on rent so that the child can have enough money for a down payment on a place of their own (which is understandable, given how high housing prices have reached in many parts of the country).

However, a significant number of young adults still living at home seem (at least outwardly) to have little incentive to find opportunities to take responsibility to support themselves. This kind of behavior doesn't just start when a child is about to graduate from high school or college. Kids do not learn to do things if things are done for them; instead, they will learn to expect others to wait on them. This may be fine when they are 2; it's not so cool at 20. So all along the way, kids need to learn to do things on their own, taking on more and more responsibilities as they grow up.

In the bestseller, *7 Habits of Highly Effective People,* Stephen Covey writes that successful people "keep the end in mind."[91] Applying that same principle to parenting is also wise. What will our children need to know how to do, and what qualities do we want them to possess as adults? Those things won't automatically happen when our children reach adulthood. They have to be taught. We don't have kids do things because we are mean, controlling, or because they are a cheap workforce; we are training them because we love them. We know that in order for them to be successful at things like holding a job, supporting a family, being happily married, and able to raise their own children, there are skills, character traits, and attitudes they need to develop.

So how do we begin preparing our children for adulthood? We can start with the basics: getting dressed; shampooing hair and washing themselves properly; cleaning bathrooms; making meals; picking up; vacuuming; dusting; washing windows and mirrors; sweeping and washing floors; doing dishes; washing and folding laundry; and so on. These are all chores that can be assigned to children. It is also amazing how much young children are really capable of doing.

Some people make the mistake of teaching their oldest child to help out and then failing to have the same expectation of their other children. This can cause anger and resentment in the oldest child. To try to avoid this, our family has made a habit of having our youngest children do chores once they are capable of doing something (such as picking up their own toys, for example), and changing or adding to their responsibilities as they get older. That way, the responsibility for each child matches what they are capable of. It is also important to explain that each person is on our "family team." We all have to work together.

As we give our children responsibilities, we do need to make sure they are trained to do these chores (remember our 4 Cs training) and that, if possible, they have the right equipment/supplies to do the chores. For very young children who are picking up toys, for example, I find it helpful both to have a "pick-up timer" (it's amazing how much they can get done in only 10 minutes) and a system in place for storing their toys, like a large basket or toy bin. This is really important because, as we all know, toys can take over a house so that even the adults can't clean it up!

If it gets to this stage, then it is time to scale down to a reasonable number of toys—this will help your kids be better able to complete their chores and will help keep your house free from clutter. Kids naturally grow out of toys; some are rarely played with, some are broken, and some are just annoying. At least once a year (if not more often), spend time with your children going through all the toys. Throw away the broken ones, bless someone else by giving away the ones that are no longer needed, and then find a place for the ones you keep.

Remember, kids won't automatically know how to do any of this unless they are taught and coached. It is helpful to work with them at first; gradually, they will be able to do all of this on their own. You must also remember that your children will follow your example; if you want your kids to pick things up daily, make sure *you* are also picking up your own things daily.

Over the years, we've found a number of things that even young children can do:

- **HELP EMPTY THE DISHWASHER.** This somewhat depends on how heavy your dishes are, but a young child can work alongside you to empty the dishwasher by stacking all the bowls or plates, for example, so that you can then put them back on the shelves. They can also put away the silverware.
- **SET OR CLEAR THE TABLE.** If your dishes are heavy or on a high shelf, take down the amount you need and place them on the counter or table for your child to set out for dinner.
- **WASH WINDOWS, OR ASSIST WITH OTHER CLEANING TASKS.** My younger kids have often loved to help me wash our windows. They also enjoy helping with dusting, holding the dust pan for sweeping, helping fold washcloths, and putting basic clothes and things away when these come out of the laundry.

As your children get older, they can begin to help with more things, such as vaccuming, dusting, sweeping floors, cleaning bathrooms, mowing the lawn, shoveling snow, vacuuming your vehicle, emptying the dishwasher, or laundry. I also have all my kids clean their room daily. These chores aren't done perfectly—particularly when my children are first learning how to do them—but the important thing is that they are being done and that the kids are learning how to do them.

In our family's experience, as the kids get older and have other paid jobs with increased responsibilities, they tend to pass their chores down to the younger kids and no longer take allowance. Interestingly, they just stop taking it themselves, without any mention of it by me or Dave. By the time they leave home, someone else has taken over their chores.

We do have allowance for our children, which varies depending on their age and what they do for chores. Each child earns a set amount per week when their chores are done; there are also extra chores the children have an option to do if they want to earn more money. They also do many things that do *not* earn them money, like helping with kitchen clean-up or general daily pick ups. Some experts say children should not be paid for chores, because chores are about teaching responsibility and learning household skills, not money. I disagree. We have seen previously in our discussions on rewards and self-centeredness that children who are given allowance without working for it become self-centered. But I find that it has worked well for my children to get an allowance for the chores they do, because they learn that work equals pay—just like in the real world—and it helps them learn valuable money- managing skills. (I will go deeper into the topic of money in Chapter 15.)

Sit down and write out the different daily and weekly chores that need to get done around your home. It is good to involve your kids so you can get their input on what things they would like to do. Figure out what you expect each child to do on a daily and/or weekly sched-ule. Then write it up so that it can be posted somewhere. I just write our kids' names and their chores underneath them on a regular piece of paper to stick on our refrigerator—as basic as it gets—but there are many downloadable chore charts available online for free.

Next, teach your kids how you want them to perform each chore. (Coaching is key!) You will need to show them and work alongside them, especially at first. Make it fun, like a game. In our house, the little ones often work alongside an older sibling when they do their chores, so they are learning from their siblings' example, and the older kids enjoy the company.

You will also need to discuss what the consequences will be if your children don't do their chores. For example, "On Fridays, we will do our chores. You will not be able to have friends over to play until they are done." Make sure you are very clear about your expectations and the consequences, but also be sure to let your kids know you are available for questions if they forget how to do something or need some assistance at the beginning. Allow for the learning time, and remember:

1. **DON'T BE CRITICAL**. Encourage them as they learn. If your kids aren't used to doing any of these things, it may take some time to learn and improve their attitude. Patience is key here.

2. **START NOW.** Even young children are capable of learning some basic chores. Give children the opportunity to learn how to help and do things. Don't wait until it is too late!

3. **GIVE ENCOURAGEMENT.** Encourage your children as they are working on a chore—not just after it is done.

4. **BE CONSISTENT**. Once a chore chart is made and explained, you must follow through and have it done weekly. Make sure you have outlined clear consequences for what will happen if chores are not completed, and then follow through with those consequences.[92]

Getting Beyond Cleaning

Learning the many basics of keeping a clean house is important, but many other tasks also teach responsibility. For example, kids can make their own breakfasts and lunches at very young ages. I usually have my children make their own by the time they are 4 years old. Usually this means getting their own cereal and milk for breakfast and then making a sandwich for their lunch. I help out at the beginning if they need it (especially with things like heavy milk jugs), but they quickly learn how to do it on their own. If your child needs a school lunch, have them make it. They will be happy to have more control over what is in it, and it is a valuable skill for them to learn. (And don't forget to teach them how they can clean up after themselves when—not if—they make a mess!)

Years ago, I gave away some unused miscellaneous things in my kitchen and cleared a space to keep some plastic bowls, plates, and cups in a low cupboard so that my young children could easily access them. Of course, I had to keep the very young 1-year-olds *out* of that cupboard because they just liked to dump all the items on the floor! But having these things in easy-to-reach places allows young children to get their dishes safely and independently and has been helpful for many years.

Pet care is another responsibility that kids can learn from a young age. Dave and I don't have a dog just to have a dog for us; we own a dog, in part, because it helps our children learn responsibility. Each child has their own task to care for our dogs, and together they do all the feeding, bathing, cleaning up after, and retrieving of them when they get out from our fenced yard. This is all part of learning responsibility. Over spring break one year, four of my younger kids took care of a friend's five pets; they divided the different tasks between them to take care of each pet—I had no part in it, other than to allow the animals into my home and to provide some supervision from a distance. It was an excellent opportunity for the kids to work, learn responsibility, enjoy the presence of having those animals around, and earn money all at the same time.

Having children pack and unpack their own school or sports bags is another important task to learn. My children pack their own swim bags, carry them to and from practice, and are responsible for putting their towels in the laundry and hanging up wet suits when we get home. They are responsible for bringing their own snack to practice; otherwise, they won't have one that day. Katie started doing this by herself at 3 years old. Asher was a bit slower, doing it at 4 years old.

If you have a fireplace, helping stock the firewood supply is another chore kids can do. All my kids haul in wood for our fireplace, even if it is only one small log at a time for the youngest kids. The younger ones go back and forth with several loads and then marvel at how much wood they brought in! There are many things that kids are capable of doing; all we have to do is train them and give them the opportunity.

Teaching the Process of Making Responsible Choices

One of the most important things a child learns is the ability to make good choices. Of course, there is a paradox to this: sometimes, too much choice is a bad thing. Barry Schwartz, an emeritus professor of psychology at Swarthmore College, did a TED talk on this very topic, where he discussed how having too many choices now causes us more stress. Just go to a grocery store to buy salad dressing, and you will see what he is talking about! All of these choices can have a paralyzing effect, and when we do eventually make a choice, often we feel less satisfied. If it isn't awesome, we imagine all the alternatives we could have chosen and feel regret and dissatisfaction.[93] So keep that in mind with our children. Our children need to be able to make their own choices, but don't overwhelm them with too many options.

For example, allow your child the ability to pick out the clothes to wear each day. It is okay to set limits—swimsuits are not to be worn to school or church, for example—but, within reason, allow your child to make their own choices. With my young children, I will give them two choices of things they can wear—two shirts, two pairs of pants, and so forth. But by the time they are 3 or so, they can dress themselves. Whatever they choose, I let them wear it! Sometimes the child's clothing choices will not match; that's okay. Sometimes, especially as they get older and I don't help at all in picking their clothes, they will be too hot or too cold. This is how they learn to make more appropriate choices—by natural consequences.

To help young children in this particular area, I like to have summer clothes accessible during the summer, and winter clothes during the winter. We also have clothes for church and clothes for playtime, and I make sure each child knows which is which, especially when they are younger. As for modesty and other clothing issues, remember you are the one who purchases clothing items. There will be a time where your children will buy their own clothes and make their own choices—you can advise them on why certain clothing choices are not a good idea, but if you haven't been teaching these things while they were young, it will be harder to have that conversation when they are adolescents and teenagers.

The Challenge of Homework

When it comes to school work, **don't** do your kids' homework for them! Kids need to learn by doing it themselves. Recently, Dave was at a swim meet where he saw a young girl working on a paper for school. The poor girl could hardly get two words written before her mother criticized her and told her how she should change the wording. It is one thing to give a couple of helpful tips after the paper is written; it's something else entirely to write it for your child. The child needs to be the one learning the skills being taught.

A few years ago, I was sitting at the orthodontist's office, and I overheard two moms talking about their issues with the middle school their children attended. One mother was indignant: "I couldn't believe it. I did *everything* on the requirement sheet for my son's science project, and he only got a B! I don't know what they expect. He also turned in a paper that my mother had gone over and made corrections on. She is an author, and he only got a B!"

I was shocked. Whose grade was it anyway—the mother's, or her son's? I couldn't help but wonder what the child was actually learning. Most likely, it wasn't the schoolwork; rather, he was learning, "I don't have to do anything; my mom will do it for me." Or perhaps he was even learning, "I am not capable of doing it myself."

It is becoming more common for parents to demand higher grades for their children—even going so far, in a few instances, to sue the school or teachers when the expected grades aren't delivered. It is true that sometimes poor grades are the result of poor teachers. But whatever happened to getting grades based on actual work, or figuring out what went wrong so that the grade on a future project will be better?

One of my sons was a procrastinator when it came to schoolwork. Even as a young child, he would do the least amount of work possible. When it came to physical work, he could go on doing things like splitting wood all day, and if he was interested in a subject, he would be better about getting his studies done. But if he *didn't* want to study a topic or complete an assignment, it was a challenge getting it done. If I didn't follow up and grade every day, he wouldn't do it. Whenever I found out he was falling behind, he would lose all play time with friends and computer time until he got caught up.

This pattern was exhausting and frustrating for me. I can't tell you how many summers my son spent doing schoolwork because of his studying choices, instead of having the summers off. I worried about this pattern when he went off to college, but I knew he would have to live with the consequences if he didn't get his work done. We are very clear with all our children from the get-go that college is a privilege; if they want our financial support for their education, they are responsible for keeping their grades up. Otherwise, they have to come up with the funds.

As I had feared, when my son went off to college, he struggled. He had to learn many tough lessons about planning ahead, how to study efficiently, and the like. About halfway through the spring semester, I got a phone call. My son's adviser was recommending he drop his calculus II class and retake it during the summer so he could focus on keeping his other grades up.

I, of course, had a number of questions for my son: "Where would you take that class? Would the credits transfer? How would that affect summer work availability?" And of course, the most important one: "How much will it cost?"

My son did not know the answers to those questions, but he said he would take responsibility for finding out the answers and that he would pay any summer school fees if he decided to go that route. After a few days, he called back and said he was not going to drop his calculus class. He had done his research; not only would it cost much more than he had anticipated, but the class wouldn't be as thorough as the one he was taking, and on top of that, he would not be able to make as much money at a summer job. So he buckled down, and with a lot of hard work, he was able to pass the class. He then worked a lot of hours all summer to contribute as much as he could to his college tuition. From then on, he was able to turn things around and do better in school.

It is hard to have your child struggle and fail, but they will—just as we have. Different kids struggle with different things, but *everyone* struggles. What we really want is for our children to struggle *well* so they can learn how to get through difficult situations and take responsibility.

Remember the Goal

As you think about chores and giving your children more responsibility, you will need to think about all the skills your children will need to live independently. They will need to know how to cook and clean; how to manage their time; how to be dependable and hard-working; how to get along with and care for others; how to handle money and plan financially for the future; and so on. These 18 years you have them under your roof are short, and there is much to learn—so start now!

When it comes to raising your children, your job is to teach *independence,* not dependence. This starts young; don't wait until your child is ready to leave for college and try to do a two-week crash course. Though that may be something that is common for many parents, it is never too late to change. Have a conversation with your family and start introducing chores into your family's daily routine. By doing so, you will begin teaching your kids *now* what they'll need to succeed as adults.

1. Recommended Reading: *Ready for Responsibility* by Bob Barnes.[94]
2. Write down the chores that need to be done.
3. Develop a chore plan/schedule and explain it to your children. It is best if you involve them in creating it. They will be happier if they have some choices about which chores they will be responsible for.
4. Once you have developed your plan, be consistent in implementing it. Don't forget to teach your children how to do what they have to do!

CHAPTER 14

Gratitude: The Key to Happiness

 PARENTING POINT: "In daily life we must see that it is not happiness that makes us grateful, but gratefulness that makes us happy."[95] Brother David Steindl-Rast, Gratefulness.org

"We have to take the twins—*now!*"

It was a shocking announcement—I had only come in for a pregnancy checkup, after all, not a full-blown delivery! There was a whirlwind of activity around me; I was quickly rolled down the hall and into an OR suite as a dozen strangers fluttered around me, gathering supplies and equipment. "Can Dave be with me?" I begged, filled with fear and concern for my babies.

"No, not now," came the reply. It was a painful response—not only because of the current circumstances, but also because of all the change our family had endured over the previous month in moving across the country to Delaware. But the ordeal would prove to be a valuable lesson for our entire family.

We had just completed a cross-country move after living near Seattle for the last five years. Dave's position in Seattle was great for his career, but the heavy travel schedule was not sustainable with six children—let alone with another set of twins on the way. He had been applying for many jobs at the corporate office in Delaware, hoping a move would reduce his travel.

Fortunately, he got a job there; unfortunately, I was 30 weeks pregnant with the twins when we had to move. To complicate things more, my twins were identical, sharing one placenta. My doctors thought the safest way for me to move would be by Amtrak train. After a 72-hour, adventure-filled train ride, we headed up to the specialist for our first OB check. The babies looked okay, so I was to have my non-stress tests and amniotic fluid checks done twice a week and would return in two weeks for my next OB appointment.

During those two weeks, we spent the first six days in a hotel, waiting to be able to close on our purchase and move into our house. The next week was spent unpacking and hiring a contractor to finish the basement so two of our sons could safely have a bedroom downstairs. In the midst of this, we had three injury mishaps during the first four days in our house. Fifteen-month-old Sophia stumbled on our sidewalk and severely scraped her forehead. Then our 7-year-old biked down our steep driveway into the cul-da-sac; he lost control and hit our neighbor's parked car. Thankfully, he was okay and our neighbor was extremely kind about the dent; it was quite the way to meet our new neighbor!

On day four, I made it very clear that we were going to take it easy— no bikes, no skateboards—because I didn't want any more injuries. I unpacked the sprinkler so the kids could still enjoy the beautiful spring day outside—until two of the boys collided and one split his knee open on a broken piece of the sprinkler. After a few stitches, things were okay. We were moved in.

The next OB appointment came; Dave and I traveled to Philadelphia to visit my doctors, leaving the kids with my mother, who thankfully had been with us for the last several weeks helping with the moving process. Dave and I met the doctor, and she decided to peek at the boys on ultrasound before sending me up to my non-stress test. Things were pretty quiet since it was Friday afternoon; all of the ultrasound technicians had already gone home.

But the mood changed as soon as the doctor started scanning my uterus. She immediately paged other doctors to come ASAP, and explained that my boys were in trouble: They had twin-to-twin-transfusion syndrome (TTTS), something I had been constantly monitored for throughout my pregnancy.

The doctors quickly decided to try stabilizing the boys by removing amniotic fluid from the baby who at this point was swimming in an ocean of it; the hope was that the other baby, who now looked like he was shrink-wrapped from a lack of amniotic fluid, would stabilize.

After what seemed like forever, two liters of fluid were drained and I was heading up to be admitted to the labor and delivery unit. The goal was to monitor the babies, give me a steroid injection to help speed up the development of their lungs before delivering them, and delay delivery for as long as possible. However, the babies were in too much distress; immediate delivery was necessary.

As I lay there, one person was taking my vital signs; another was starting an IV; the anesthesiologist was next in line to give me my epidural; the draping cloth was raised as my doctor prepped my abdomen for the C-section. I asked several times if my husband could come in, but I knew they were busy trying to save my children's lives. As they were lifting Levi out of my abdomen, Dave was allowed to come in. Luke was born a minute later, and both boys were whisked to the NICU to be intubated. It would be eight long hours before I would get to see them for the first time, and a month before they were able to come home.

As stressful as those weeks and months were, they were filled with gratitude and a peace that only God can give. My husband had a job, one that would allow him to be home at night instead of traveling during these hectic months. We had a warm and protective home for our family. I had a husband who loved me. Luke and Levi's delivery was hardly as we had hoped, but they were alive and doing well, other than normal issues for their age and size. Things were not easy, but it was going to be okay.

Over the years, many people have wondered how I can juggle and cope with having 10 children. There have been unbelievably challenging situations, but there were two things that sustained me through all of them: God and gratitude. I knew God was there with me and would help me get through each challenge, so I prayed often. Feeling and knowing his presence gave great comfort. I also made a point to try and live a life of gratitude for what we had. We often can't control our circumstances, but we can control both our attitude and our response to those dark moments. I tried very hard to focus on the positives, the things in each circumstance I could be thankful for.

In this country, it's easy for us to take a lot for granted. Most of us have homes with an array of food available; we have an abundance of clean water and structured sewer systems that effectively remove waste at the flush of a toilet; we have electricity and refrigeration; we have stoves, dishwashers, and washing machines to help make our work around the home a little easier. We have freedom to practice our religions openly and largely without restriction or fear. We have access to transportation, which is often equipped with videos, music, air-conditioning, and plenty of storage. Many of us are able to own a variety of electronics, and we have access to cable and internet that can connect us to people all around the world.

Yet, there is so much discontent. Why is that? Why are so many lottery winners more miserable after winning than before? Why are many famous and wealthy people struggling with addictions and relationships and repeatedly in trouble with the law?

We live in the richest nation in history, yet research repeatedly shows that Americans are growing less and less pleased with life. Psychologists at the University of Liege studied the idea of *experience-stretching*—that is, the notion that when we have an experience, that same experience doesn't give us the same satisfaction as it did the first time. By enjoying the best things in life, like nice trips, great food, or the newest gadgets, we actually decrease our ability to enjoy the mundane joys of everyday life.[96]

The rapidly changing pace of our technology is a huge contributor to this discontent. Technology is changing so rapidly that only a few months after your purchase, something new and better comes out, and sometimes for less money. Discontent becomes commonplace.

We are also bombarded by advertising meant to make us want something we don't have. An advertisement's goal is to make us feel discontent and have the fear of missing out, so that we buy the item in question. We continue spending more and more money but never feel satisfied.

Maybe this doesn't happen in your house—if so, tell me your secrets!—but I have noticed that my kids will be so excited to get a particular Lego set that they just *have* to have. Once the gift is opened and the must-have Lego set is put together, they go right back to the computer to see what they want next!

The same is true for me. That desire to get one thing or another may drive me to purchase something, but most times, it really isn't that satisfying once I have it. That desire is a crazy monster that is never satisfied, no matter how much it is fed. Happiness is not found in the accumulation of material things.

Joshua Fields Millburn and Ryan Nicodemus, whose blog is called "The Minimalists,"[97] found contentment when they *got rid* of most of their material belongings. As a result of their story, many others are finding contentment when they get rid of most of their material things.

Interestingly, the Amish are a group of people who continue to score high on the happiness scale. They also have a significantly lower depression and suicide rate. Instead of valuing material possessions, they value relationships, family, their community, and God, and they practice gratitude.[98]

There are a number of benefits to practicing a life of gratitude:[99] [100]

1. Better health
2. Better sleep[101]
3. Less anxiety and depression
4. Increased kindness, decreased aggression
5. Happier disposition

6. Closer relationships
7. Better grades

As with so many things, it's easy to say, "I want to live a life of gratitude." But how do we *do* this? And how can it impact our parenting?

Ways to Develop an Attitude of Gratitude

Over the years, our family has found a number of ways to practice living a life centered around gratitude. Some of the following examples are from those experiences, while others are rooted in research.

WRITE A THANK YOU NOTE OR VISIT SOMEONE YOU'RE GRATEFUL FOR. In one study, a "gratitude visit"—that is, writing a thank-you letter and taking it or mailing it to someone—increased a happiness score by 10 percent![102] Think about someone who changed your life for the better. Take the time to write a letter to that person and thank them.

I did this years ago to my fifth-grade teacher. I was sick a lot that year and missed quite a bit of school. She was always kind to me, and I appreciated that so much. She was also the person who introduced me to the Little Britches books by Ralph Moody, which have become our favorite family read-alouds. So, I wrote to her and thanked her—even though I had had no contact with her since fifth grade! My parents had moved from Wisconsin to Arizona when I was 18, so the town where I grew up was a place I no longer even visited. But I went through the effort to find my teacher's address and then wrote her the letter. She was so sweet and wrote me back, and we have now been corresponding annually with our Christmas letters for more than a decade.

Take the time to write to that person in *your* life! Not only should we reach out to those around us and personally thank them, but we should teach our children to do the same, both verbally and with written thank-you cards. Even the simplest notes or expressions of gratitude can make such a difference.

KEEP A GRATITUDE JOURNAL. The best way to have a life of gratitude is to intentionally live each day with a heart of gratitude. One way is to start a gratitude journal. Studies show that a gratitude journal had the longest lasting and most significant effect on a person's happiness; in fact, this happiness level continued to increase for six months! Intentionally cultivating gratitude has a positive effect on our mental health.

To write a gratitude journal, write three things each day for which you are grateful. It can be anything, from the taste of creamy ice cream, to rain quenching the dry grass, to children playing together nicely in the next room. This process of writing down such gifts every day will keep your mind focused on the lovely mundane things that we often miss, overlook, or take for granted. We need to set the example and have our children write a gratitude journal as well. You can also implement saying three things we are grateful for at dinner time and/or at bedtime. For more depth on this topic, please read Ann Voskamp's book, *One Thousand Gifts: A Dare to Live Fully Right Where You Are.*

FOSTER RELATIONSHIPS IN YOUR FAMILY. Spend time developing relationships with your children and significant other, rather than just buying them things. Our children's fondest memories aren't of any big extravagant item we purchased, but rather of running relay races with our family in the yard, playing charades, and taking day trips to the beach or hiking.

Our dissatisfaction rubs off on our children; so does our gratitude. Do our children always hear us talk about how we want a bigger house, nicer furniture, or any number of our other wants, or do they hear us being grateful in our prayers and speech throughout the day? Do we grumble about everything our spouse *doesn't* do, or do we speak about all that we are glad he or she *does* do? Do we complain about all that our children do wrong, or do we make sure to acknowledge the things we appreciate about each one? Are we looking at life as though the cup is half empty or half full?

REMEMBER THE POWER OF 'GOOD ENOUGH.'[103] Someone will always have a bigger, nicer house with nicer furniture, nicer vehicles, and nicer gadgets. Instead of focusing on this reality, be grateful for what you do have and recognize that an item's value might not be in its monetary worth.

I have found that my least expensive, free, or second-hand items have the best stories behind them, making them very valuable to me. For example, we have an old desk that used to belong to the sister of one of my friends in Seattle. When we moved to Delaware, we didn't really have a place for it, and so we set it out for a charity to pick up, but they refused it. Into the garage it went.

Just weeks later, when Luke and Levi came home from the hospital, we needed a place to change their diapers. My mother-in-law, who was visiting, suggested we paint the old desk, put new knobs on it, and then use that. Thirteen years later, we *still* use it; it actually looks pretty cool, almost like something you would find at Pottery Barn, but at one point, I couldn't even give it away!

Our house is filled with items like this—items that have a unique story and great value to us. Sure, it would be nice to buy new, matching furniture, but even if I had the money, at this point, I doubt I would spend it that way. We have more than enough to be grateful for amongst our possessions, and there are many other important things to spend our finances on.

ATTEND RELIGIOUS SERVICES. Spirituality and gratitude are linked. Those who attend a church service regularly have more gratitude.[104] Martin Luther referred to gratitude as "the basic Christian attitude." Because Christians believe they should praise and thank God for all he has given and done, gratitude is at the core. People who attend church often have a deeper relationship with God. And those with a deeper relationship with God have a deeper sense of gratitude.

SERVE OTHERS. Chapter 12 addresses this topic.

READ BOOKS. Read books aloud to your children, past the age when they can read themselves. Read aloud, chapter books—both fiction and non-fiction—open up the lives of those past and present who often faced extreme hardships. For example, when we read *A Long Walk to Water* by Linda Sue Park or *Running for My Life* by Lopez Lomong, my children saw a glimpse into the extreme trials those in Sudan have endured in recent history, as well as problems the Sudanese currently face. They also learned how these authors survived and overcame these challenges, and how they are using their current situations to raise awareness and give back to the people of Sudan. We tend to take clean water and political stability for granted, but reading these books opens our eyes to others in the world who struggle for these same basic necessities. It helps develop gratitude for what we have and empathy for others.

Life doesn't always give us what we hope or plan for, but gratitude in our circumstances helps us feel peace and happiness. A year ago, my son lost his job when the company he was working for was having financial problems. He and his wife had just bought their first home, and his wife was pregnant with their second child. With no severance package, a family to support, and the need to sell their home and find a job quickly, many people would have been in despair. However, I saw that my son focused on creating an action plan and living out his life with gratitude. He was grateful he had his college degree and a loving wife, and he was optimistic that things would work out in the long run.

Eventually things did—though not exactly in the way we had expected. Instead of my son getting a job closer to family, a job opportunity came up in Florida—more than 15 hours of driving away. After they moved, it took a long 10 months to sell their house, so they lived in a tiny apartment, paying both their mortgage and rent all that time. But because of my son's lens of gratitude, he talks about being grateful for his new job, what he has learned, and how he hopes to advance. He talks about how with their budget, they have been able to weather this period of financial difficulty; now, with the house sold, they can start saving toward owning a home again in the future. They miss family, and we miss them, but they are enjoying spending time in the sun and being at the beach. My grandson loves seeing the "tee tees" (manatees) at the aquarium. There were times last year when my son ate tuna, rice, and beans for every lunch and dinner. It was cheap and filling, but he had food. About a month after that, during the move, his new company gave them a food allowance, so they got to eat at restaurants. He was grateful in both circumstances. This isn't the last trial they will face, but I know my son and his family have the attitude, gratitude, and resilience to get through future challenges.

Practicing an attitude of gratitude will increase our happiness, promote mental and physical health, build closer relationships, and help us improve our productivity. In this world of material things, let's be grateful for what we have, not longing for all the things we don't. By practicing an attitude of gratitude and intentionally teaching it to our children, they will learn to be grateful as well.

1. Start a gratitude journal along with your children.
2. Practice saying positive things and stop when you hear yourself being critical. It will rub off on your children and others around you.
3. Practice being content with what you have.
4. Write thank you notes and have your children do the same.

CHAPTER 15

Financial Training: Using Money Wisely

 PARENTING POINT: Parents are the number one influencers regarding money.

Money: The topic that most people never want to talk about. When they do, it often makes them angry or frustrated. Yet this is one of the most important subjects you need to teach your children about. The hard thing about parenting is that sometimes when we want to teach our children to do the right thing, we have to take an honest look at our own choices. People at all income levels can "be broke" (spending more than they have), but people with much lower levels of income than others can be much more financially stable. The key is how you handle the money you have.

Managing finances is one of the most important skills our children need to learn—and yet it's one that we so rarely teach. Parenting expert Bob Barnes makes a great point about this. When you teach your child to drive, do you hand him the car keys the day he turns 16 and say, "Good luck?" Of course not! So, if all that preparation goes into driving, why don't we do the same preparation for teaching children about money?[105] It's time we teach our children about dollars and sense.

How are our kids doing with financial literacy? The Jumpstart Coalition for Personal Financial Literacy conducted surveys from 1997-2008. On a 31-question financial literacy exam, the average score in 1997 was 57.3 percent; that average *dropped* to 48.3 percent in 2008.[106] On the 2015 National Report Card on State Efforts to Improve Financial Literacy in high schools, only five states scored an A for requiring a semester of a personal finance course; nearly a quarter of states received an F because they had absolutely no financial literacy requirements at all.[107]

It probably won't surprise you to learn that high school students who take a personal finance class are more likely to save money and pay off their credit card bills in full each month, and they are less likely to be compulsive buyers or max-out their credit cards. Those statistics are even better when kids start learning about money in kindergarten or first grade.

In order to make wise financial decisions, your child needs a solid education in financial literacy. As with most of life's skills, parents are shown to have the most influence on a child's financial literacy, so make this a priority! The best way for children to learn is to practice making financial choices. This surprises or even frightens many people: "Give a child money? They'll waste it on useless items! Or what if they lose it? No, no, I will just get them what they need."

Do you think your kids will magically know how to manage money when they graduate from high school, or when they are in college, or when they have their first job after college, simply because they will be older? In fact, so many people struggle with credit card debt and other financial problems precisely because they *didn't* learn how to manage money before they were responsible for making big financial decisions. Those financial decisions they make when deciding on which college they should attend and how to finance it, what car they want to buy, which apartment they want to rent or house they want to own, and so on are all likely to come immediately after high school graduation; teaching sound financial principals cannot be delayed.

It is better for our children to make financial mistakes and learn when they are young and the stakes are not quite so high than to assume that they will learn when they get older. It is much better for them to buy a remote-control helicopter that breaks the first day and learn the lesson about buying something very fragile at 10 years old than to buy a used car without careful inspection at 25 and find out it needs a new transmission. They can make life-altering mistakes as adults—burying themselves in credit card debt or other debt, earning poor credit ratings, building no savings, and failing to pay their bills on time.

This is why we need to make sure we teach and guide our kids in making sound financial decisions by giving them opportunities to participate in the three S's of finance: spending, saving, and sharing. But before we can get to those three steps, first we must talk about the ways our children can and should earn their money.

Earning

The process begins when we give our children opportunities to earn money by doing work, just as they will as adults. In our house, our kids have to help around the house and complete chores to receive their weekly allowance, which varies depending on their age.

Now, many experts advise against paying children for chores but recommend an allowance. Personally, this makes no sense to me. Do the children still get an allowance if they don't complete their chores? If not, how does this system differ from paying your children for doing their chores? If so, then how does this teach them about the real-world process of working to earn money? Of course, you will have to decide what system works for your own family.

Our kids have many daily and weekly chores. They receive their allowance after their big weekly chores are done, but they don't ask for money each time I ask them to do something. Helping around the house is an expectation for being part of the family, and daily chores like making their beds, helping clean the kitchen, and pet care are expected but not rewarded. Also, chores are not optional in our house. Our kids have to do their chores before they can play with friends or have time on the computer. Weekly allowance in our family ranges from one-to-ten dollars, depending on the age of the child and how many chores they do. If they want to earn more money, I have other chores they can do in addition to their weekly chores. They also get money for birthday or Christmas gifts.

As your kids get older, encourage entrepreneurship as they seek new ways to earn money. In our last neighborhood, word spread that my kids could be called to move furniture, spread mulch, mow lawns, and shovel snow.

During the years with a lot of snow, they used only shovels, and they started thinking about how many more driveways they could do if they had a snow blower (not to mention how much easier the work would be!). So my kids made a deal with Dave. Dave would buy a snow blower for them, and they would put at least half of their earnings for each driveway they cleared toward repaying the cost until they had completely repaid him. The kids worked very hard that winter, and put most of their earnings into repaying Dave so they could clear their debt. At the end of that first winter, they were excited—they had paid off the snow blower, so the next winter they could keep all their earnings as profit.

Unfortunately, the next winter, it didn't snow; no snow blower was needed. It was certainly disappointing to our kids, but it was a tremendous lesson for them. They worked hard, fulfilled their responsibility to pay off the debt to expand their business, and then their asset—the snow blower—wasn't useful the next year. That can happen with any business, but it was a lesson they learned when the stakes were smaller; a snow blower is not nearly as costly as an entire business.

In the warmer months, a couple of my boys mowed neighbor's lawns. One of them wanted a zero-turn mower so he could do a more professional job with his mowing. So, when our lawn mower broke and needed to be replaced, he put $500 toward the new one Dave was buying so that he could have the zero-turn mower he wanted. It was a great investment idea and another excellent lesson learned.

I cannot stress enough the importance and value of jobs for teens. It's true that some teens don't *need* to have a job to earn money because of their parents' affluence; it's also true that many teens are busy with sports and other extracurricular activities. However, if they don't have a job in their teen years, kids will miss out on one of the best opportunities for their future. When they apply for a job, they have their first experience searching for a job, creating a resume or filling out an application, and interviewing for a position. They have to learn how to dress and act in an interview. They may even experience *not* getting the job they apply for—an unfortunate but important experience to have for dealing with that same process as an adult.

Once they have a job, they will learn how to work under a boss who isn't a parent; they will have to figure out how to deal with co-workers; they will learn what it means to be accountable for their work; they will experience doing tasks that are new and uncomfortable. But as time goes by, they will become more confident and proficient.

There are so many other skills and experiences that working as a teenager provides. These early jobs may teach them what they *don't* want to do when they are an adult and can motivate them to pursue something else. They learn the crucial life skills of planning ahead and learning time management. My kids have to submit for time off weeks ahead of schedule or find a replacement so they can get certain days off. There have been times they have failed to do this and have had to miss something they wanted to do because they had to go to work.

These early work experiences can also provide hard, humbling, and character-forming moments. My children have forgotten to set alarms and have been late to work because they did not wake up in time, forcing them to admit their failure to their bosses and apologize. Situations like these aren't comfortable, but it's important to experience them and learn from them, even at an early age.

Additionally, when teens earn money themselves, that money has a much higher value to them than if it had just been given to them. They realize how many hours have to be worked to earn enough money to buy things. They see how taxes are taken out, and they learn how to file for a refund in the spring. They experience how to handle money of their own. Teens who may not financially "need" a job are probably the ones who need this hands-on experience the most.

Spend

Once our kids have begun earning even a little bit of money, we must help them understand what it means to spend their hard-earned money responsibly. Even in this digital era, when it comes to spending, cash is the best method for this kind of education. Many experts teach that even adults who are struggling financially should adopt a cash system. By using cash, your kids can learn how to handle, count, and take responsibility for their money. There's also something about the physical reality of holding money; when a child hands over a bundle of cash earned over many weeks of hard work, it's a different reality than if they had just used a virtual payment.

One of the most important aspects about handling money is teaching how to store it responsibly. We usually give a wallet or purse to a young child as a birthday present when we start giving an allowance for chores. Even so, it is not uncommon for young children, or any children not used to handling their own money, to lose it. Do *not* replace lost money. This is a significant moment for a child to learn how to become responsible in handling money.

Once your children have begun earning their own money, moments where they ask for you to buy something become opportunities to teach them: It is wonderful! Usually by the time they are 5 years old, my kids have really started to keep track of their money and saving for things they want. When you are at the checkout line in a store and your child asks if she can get some candy, say, "No, I am not going to buy you those things anymore. You have your own money now, so if you want something, you can save your money, bring your wallet, and buy it with your money." You can then explain how much she earns each week and how much whatever she wanted costs. The child then starts to associate value to items, and it gives her some control.

When they begin paying for things with their own finances, children realize that items have value; they learn what it means to have to work toward a goal of buying something; they better understand what it means to be the owner of an item; they realize the value of time as it relates to earning money.

At that point, they start to make wiser financial choices: Do I want to buy that small thing now, or wait and get something I *really* want later? They won't learn this right away; when they spend their money on something small like a candy bar, they learn that they will not have enough for one of their larger wish-list items. When kids first start receiving money, they usually want to spend whatever they receive, but over time, they will learn that if they want something else, they will have to save first.

When you start giving your children money and then visit a store, it is good to talk about things they've said they want to buy ahead of time. You can help them through the thinking process, but it is still important to allow *them* to make financial decisions. Yes, they will spend it foolishly; haven't we all? Dave and I have watched our kids spend money on things we know will break immediately, but they were *sure* they wanted those things. When the inevitable happens and the item breaks, the kids feel remorse for blowing all that hard-earned money on something that didn't last. But experience is the best teacher, and they learn through natural consequences. Again, it's much better if this happens to them when they are younger, because the stakes are not as high.

Starting in middle school, our kids are responsible for paying for half of the cost of church-related activities, including retreats and local mission trips. If they want to go on an international mission trip, they earn all the money needed to go; we only pay for the passport. We believe that children should earn their money through work, not by asking for donations from friends and relatives. They pay for all their entertainment expenses or extras they want, like movies, fast foods, computers or other electronics. They have to save and budget so they have the money they need for the more expensive items.

Remember, we are teaching responsibility by having our children handle money. Part of responsibility is that the child learns through consequences and the parent doesn't bail them out all the time. For example, Dave and I provide the swimsuits, goggles, towels, kick boards, and pull-buoys for our kids' swim team training. Over time, as things wear out or are outgrown, we pay to replace those. However, if a child forgets something and loses it at the pool, then it is *his* responsibility to pay to replace the item. This has happened several times, and each time, the child has painfully had to purchase the lost item. However, our kids have learned over the years to be responsible with their equipment.

My kids pay for school books in college and learn how to shop for the best deal. They also figure out how to sell the books in the spring to recoup some of their money. They have also learned that if their books have not been well-cared for, their value is significantly less. Some of my kids worked part-time while in college, and some have had to make their summer earnings stretch the whole school year. I do not send any "allowance" or money for my kids in college. They learn how to handle money in high school and do a great job of learning how to budget in college. These are natural progressions; when they graduate, they have the knowledge, skills, and discipline to handle money as adults.

Save

Saving is the second "S" in finances, and it is one that we can start modeling to our kids before they are even aware of it. When each of my children was born, we opened up a savings account with money given to the child as a gift. If you have not done so yet, I encourage you to open up a basic savings account for each of your kids. It's true that your children will not earn much for many years, which may make a savings account something that is rarely used. But it is important that children know what such an account is and how it benefits them, even when they are young. Even in elementary school, it can be an important lesson; one of my sons has been saving his weekly allowance for so long that he put quite a bit into his savings account. Dave and I do not have a mandatory savings process for our young children, but I have found they all learn to save by knowing they have the option available to them. The saving becomes their choice and has carried them into adulthood with solid financial principles. When my teens start earning more consistent money through jobs, the savings account becomes very useful. They can direct deposit their money into their account and start accessing it through a debit card. Ultimately, what our teens spend their money on is their choice, but we do make sure to have a conversation about how much they think would be reasonable to spend versus how much they need to save for college costs or other big expenses in the future. I do not micromanage their accounts because they have to learn to do this on their own.

Once another mother told me, "Oh, my son is a great saver. He doesn't spend a thing." When I asked her more about it, I found out she bought everything he wanted. So, of course he was a great saver; he had no reason to spend his money! Buying an abundance of things for your children—especially when they have money of their own to spend—has the opposite effect of what you want them to learn. Those material things become of little value, and you have robbed your child of the satisfaction that comes from delayed gratification, hard work, and the ability to be in control of their own money.

Sharing

The final S that we must teach our kids is "sharing," or giving. Now that they have an income, they will have an opportunity to learn how to give some of it away. How you teach this opportunity will depend on your individual family; some families require their children to set aside a certain amount for giving, but Dave and I have decided to set an example of generosity for our kids, instead of requiring it of them.

Some of the kids are natural tithers (giving 10 percent of what they earn to God). One of our sons has tithed for as long as I can remember; most of it has gone to church, but he has also given money for other charitable causes and nonprofits he's passionate about. Another son has loaned to people around the world through Kiva.org, as well as Smile

Train. A third son has spent much of his money to go on mission trips with the youth group and gives generously while there.

This spirit of giving has continued in our younger children as well. When Sophia was 5, she gave all of her allowance to her Sunday school class during their fundraiser to help free modern-day slaves in India. She knew that they needed the money more than she did. She also wanted to teach Luke and Levi, who were 4 at the time, to give, so she gave part of her own allowance money to them so they could also "give" it away.

When we sponsored another child through Compassion International, I was showing the kids his picture. They asked if they could give to him as well, and when I said they could give whatever they wanted, they got so excited that they ran upstairs, pooled their money together, and donated $32 to him. The kids were 6 and 7 years old at the time. Had they not been given an allowance or been trained to save it, they would not have had the opportunity to experience the joy of giving in that situation.

When your children learn to give to others, it can also improve their relationships with each other. It brings tears to my eyes when I watch my kids' generosity to each other at Christmas. Oftentimes, my teens come home with food they have bought and openly share it with their siblings. When my kids see needs, they are compelled to help. By modelling a spirit of giving and allowing them to give from their hearts, I have seen lasting effects in my children.

Remember, these values are caught, not taught. We need to have a giving heart and be generous with all that we have.

Moving Beyond the Basics

As children get older, they need to be allowed to make more financial choices. They need to understand debt, credit, the high cost of credit card debt, how credit cards work, and the difference between credit cards and debit cards. They need to understand what a credit rating is and how it affects them; they need to understand interest rates, the ancillary costs of certain items (such as costs of vehicle maintenance and insurance in addition to the purchase price of a vehicle, tax, and licensure). They need to learn the importance of budgeting, so it is great for them to see your budget so they can better understand the cost of things like a mortgage, electricity, phone, internet, water, and sewer services, as well as how to read bills.

And then there are things like insurance—what do you need, what will it cover, and how much will it cost? How much food do you need to buy each week? How much should you save for emergencies? For vacations? For retirement?

These are not things that can easily be taught or learned in one sitting. Be open and honest with your kids, providing more information and specifics as they get older. Teach them the benefits and dangers of all these things and more—and be sure you learn them yourself! Don't think that someone else is going to teach them these lessons. People experiencing financial messes (as a result of poor financial choices, job loss, or unexpected and expensive medical bills) would likely have benefited from gaining more knowledge, restraint, and accountability early in their lives.

One way to teach your children better financial principles is to outline a few for your family to follow. The key financial principles that have helped us immensely are:

1. Don't buy anything unless you have the cash to pay for it fully— including vehicles. (A house is the exception.)
2. Work to pay off all debt as soon as possible.
3. Save for retirement and emergencies that come up.
4. Be a generous giver.

You may be looking at your own finances and saying, "I've messed up myself. I don't have a handle on this; how can I teach this to my children?" I encourage you to study this topic, have some good conversations with your spouse or significant other, and take a hard look at your own finances. If you find yourself in an unusual or difficult life circumstance, this is not meant to be an indictment. Make steps to get back on your feet again.

I would highly recommend taking courses like a Financial Peace Class or finding resources to help you make better financial choices. It is okay to be honest and teach your kids what you have learned from the mistakes you have made. Doing so will help in your life, which will in turn affect your children. Teaching your children about money now can prevent financial mistakes when the stakes are high as adults.

1. Take a look at your own finances and seek guidance through books or classes if needed.
2. Develop a plan for your children to earn money.
3. Start teaching your children about finances and allowing them to handle money.

CHAPTER 16

Teaching Spirituality: Will You Let Your Child Decide?

PARENTING POINT: Parents' example impacts children the most.

There is a broad spectrum of parent opinion regarding spiritual teaching for kids; many people consider this extremely important, and many don't. Among those who don't believe guidance in spiritual matters is important, their apathy can stem from a lack of conviction in their own faith or simply an insecurity about how to teach their children. About a third of the kids in the youth group at our church have parents who do not attend church themselves. Don't get me wrong, attending youth group, Sunday school, or other church-related activities is great for kids and teens, and I know they can glean a lot on their spiritual journey from these activities; however, your children will experience far greater benefit if *you* are on this spiritual journey with them.

When it comes to spirituality, some parents take a hands-off approach: "Oh, we just want to let our children decide. We don't want to force anything on them." But do we do this with other aspects of their lives?

Do we just let our children decide what to eat because we don't want to force fruit and vegetables on them? Do we just let kids learn whatever they want, because we don't want to force math and reading on them? Of course not. We guide and train them because we have more wisdom and know what is best for them down the road (even if we aren't fans of broccoli or algebra!). If we have strong personal convictions about faith and spirituality—especially for those of us who have a mandate from the Bible to teach the next generation—then we must understand that it's important for us to encourage the development of spirituality in our children's lives.

I realize everyone comes from varying religious backgrounds; some of our homes were extremely religious, while others were more moderate or non-religious. A common challenge couples face is the experience of having grown up in different religious backgrounds. No matter what happened in the past or what we have done so far with our kids, we need to be honest with ourselves and our significant others. Then, we need to decide what our goals are and take responsibility for how we are guiding our children spiritually. Because I am Christian, I will be mostly discussing matters of Christian spirituality—but establishing a strong religious foundation at home applies across all faiths.

Why Christians Focus on Teaching Spirituality and Faith

For those of the Christian faith, chances are very high that a child raised in a Christian home, but without any spiritual guidance, will not choose to follow Jesus as an adult. It can happen, but chances are statistically low. According to the Nazarene Church Growth Research, 85 percent of people accepted Christ between the ages of 4 and 14. Another 10 percent accepted Christ between the ages of 15 and 30 years old, and only four percent did so after the age of 30.[108] Because childhood years are so important for laying a strong spiritual foundation, we need to take this task seriously.

Children have a natural enthusiasm for matters of faith. I see this excitement and enthusiasm in my younger kids, who love to learn about Scripture and ask a lot of questions. They openly talk about their faith and are puzzled when their friends don't believe in God. Some of their questions are *hard*, like, "If God created everything, who created God?"

Second Timothy 3:14-17 (NIV) says, "But as for you, continue in what you have learned and have become convinced of, because you know those from whom you learned it, and how *from infancy* you have known the Holy Scriptures, which are able to make you wise for salvation through faith in Christ Jesus. All Scripture is God-breathed and is useful for teaching, rebuking, correcting, and training in righteousness, so that the man of God may be thoroughly equipped for every good work" (emphasis added). Paul speaks as someone who was a religious leader in the Jewish culture: In their culture then (and in many kinds of Judaism now), it was very important for Jewish children to learn the Scriptures—what Christians refer to as the Old Testament—from an early age. Paul knew the value of knowing Scripture and exploring faith from childhood, and it is just as important for us today.

According to a Pew Research survey on religious preference, the results showed that of those survey respondents who were born before 1928, only five percent were *not* affiliated with a religion. With each generation after that, a larger percentage was not affiliated with a religion. The generation who was least affiliated with a religion was the millennials, at 26 percent.[109]

There are also some sobering statistics for children who were raised in a church and active in the youth group. Depending on the study you examine, anywhere from 50 to 90 percent of these kids will not stay active in church once they enter college. However, some of those who left will come back to church as they settle down with families. The numbers do trend downward, though, showing that more and more people consider themselves atheist, agnostic, or unsure. I personally want nothing more than to spend eternity with my husband and children, so helping my children develop and grow in their faith is a priority for me. This means we must pay attention to where we place God in our own lives: is he front and center, or is he on the sidelines? How we live out our faith provides the example for our children to follow.

There are various reasons that youth leave their religious upbringing. Some find church boring or irrelevant. They feel it ignores their real-world problems and is too negative about current movies, music, and media. Some think the tenets of Christian faith contradict science and lack evidence.[110] Others felt judged or didn't feel their faith was working for them[111] or was vague. Never personally owning their faith or simply having other priorities also leads to their departure from Christianity.

For those teens who go to college, about 25 percent of their professors will be professing atheists or agnostics; 51 percent of professors describe the Bible as "a book of fables, legends, history, and moral precepts."[112] Some secular colleges and universities also avoid any religious display and seem hostile toward religion. One student I know went to a university which didn't allow any Christmas decorations at all, including Christmas lights on campus, even within their on-campus housing. There are even 224 affiliate Secular Student Alliance groups in high schools, colleges and universities across the US which promote and proselytize *un*belief. However, even though believing young people are not guaranteed to find believing mentors outside of the homes and home churches once they move out and into adulthood, that support *does* exist if it is sought. I would also say that for one of my sons, even though the percent of students who identified as Christian on his campus were small, they held very strong beliefs and were an incredible support.

What can we do to help beliefs and faith to hold fast? There are a number of ways that we can raise our children to help them develop a solid faith rooted in the truth of Christ's love.

Parental Modeling

How you express and live out your faith may have a greater impact on your son or daughter than any other factor in their lives.[113] That can be good news or bad news. There are some parents who drop their kids off at church and allow them to attend confirmation class, youth group, or a Sunday school class, but they do not attend church or have a relationship with Christ themselves. This kind of attitude sends a message to our children: "God is not important for me, but you should go." This is not effective in helping our children develop strong spiritual lives. However, those college students who kept their faith said that when they had doubts or questions, the first thing they did was talk to their parents or read their Bibles.[114]

Children are more likely to follow their parents' beliefs if they see and hear them making a difference in their parents' lives. It is not too late to take action. Setting the example of reading Scripture yourself and with your children, teaching them to do it themselves, discussing your thoughts about it, and sharing prayer requests all provide opportunities to connect with your children as well as grow your faith. Your spiritual journey is a life-long process, and so is theirs. It is also not too early. Start now—wherever you are—and move forward.

One of the things we most need to model is an unconditional, non-judgmental, and ever-embracing love that our kids can do nothing to jeopardize or even lessen. We must take the path of expressing our love when they make big or small mistakes, whether they are following our lead or not. "There's nothing you can do to make me love you more and nothing you can do to make me love you less."[115] The void of not feeling this unconditional love can send people down destructive paths. Life is filled with many ups and downs; if your children feel your unconditional love and that you believe in them, especially during difficult times, it will make an enormous difference for them and for you. If they have strayed from their faith during those challenging seasons, they are also more likely to return to it if their parents have been tolerant, open, and loving during times of doubt and questioning.

A survey of 500 college students by the Fuller Institute found that when a student made a poor choice in the first two weeks of college, they felt they had messed up, so it was too late to change.[116] However, the message that needs to ring clearly is that they are loved—by us and by God, not because of what they do or don't do. We all mess up and fall short, but that is not the end of the story. God does not abandon us when we mess up, but is waiting with open arms. Because Jesus died on the cross, we have forgiveness. His love and grace are gifts; they are not earned.

God loves us unconditionally, which is how we must love our children. Do your kids know that you are there for them no matter what? Do we show our love through the majors and the minors, big and small challenges? Do your kids know that Jesus is there for them, no matter what? (See Chapter 4 for more depth about how to show love.)

Attending Church Services Together

There is a direct relationship between a child's attendance at church-wide worship services and the development of a faith that continues into adulthood.[117] This means that the children of families who attend corporate worship together have a higher probability of keeping their faith when they grow up.

When I talk with parents about keeping their kids—even their young kids—in the regular service with them at church, as opposed to sending them to Sunday school or other child-oriented programming during that time, I often hear reasons why parents don't want to do that:

- "My kids don't sit still."
- "The service is boring for kids."
- "I need a break from my kids."
- "My kids are too distracting."
- "They are getting all they need from Sunday school."

Some of these sound like valid reasons—particularly the last one—but research shows that a child's attendance at a church's regular worship service makes a difference in the long-term impact of their faith development. And when we think about it, it makes sense—after all, if their only experience is Sunday school and youth group, what will make them want to attend church as an adult? It is foreign to them. It is not familiar or part of their regular habit, and thus it is easier to let church attendance fade away from their regular routine. Ben, my 23-year-old, said that after having church as part of his life since birth, it would have felt odd if he didn't go to church in college. Establishing this as a habit will create an environment where your children can grow spiritually, regardless of the situations they encounter. As they mature, they need to develop their own relationship with Christ.

Our kids have experienced so much by worshiping with Dave and I over the years. To be clear, our children have also attended Sunday school and youth group, and they have enjoyed it; since they are home-schooled, this has been an important social outlet for my kids. But, as I mentioned earlier, research has shown that children are more likely to develop a "sticky faith" that endures over the long-term if they attend a church's main worship service with their parents. Dave and I have handled this in our family by attending the worship service together and then having kids go to Sunday school during the second service. This also gives Dave and I an opportunity to serve, as we often teach a Sunday school class while our kids are in their classes.

Additionally, we have always brought our new babies into church with us, stepping out if they became noisy. We used the nursery for some of the children when they were little, but by the time they were 2 or 3 years old, all our children were back in the service with us. As our eight boys and two girls have grown, they have learned to sit quietly and worship with us in church. I have found that they do much better if we sit near the front (but not the first row because they need the containment of the seats in front of them!) By sitting near the front, they can see better and there are fewer distractions. We have also minimized the things we bring in to keep them occupied; in our experience, the more food or toys we brought in, the noisier they were. If they don't want to pay attention or are too young to sit still and listen for that long, it is best to have them sit quietly and draw on the bulletin instead of bringing other things into the service.

Dave and I have continually noticed benefits to having our children in the service with us. Even when it appears they aren't paying attention, they bring something up later that was talked about in the sermon. For kids who are not as verbal or outgoing, you may not always hear or witness that they are engaged, but in our experience, they *are* absorbing it. Having our kids in church has allowed them to learn, understand, and take part in the life of the church community. It has never been optional; instead, it's an expectation every Sunday (unless they have an illness). To us, giving back one morning a week to worship God is a very small thing. It isn't a chore; nor is it a duty. It is part of who we are, as children of God, to be in fellowship and worship God each week, and it is communicated as such to our family.

Mentorship

Intergenerational relationships are an important aspect of training your children sensibly and spiritually. As shown by the research at Fuller Institute, having a 5:1 ratio is very important. This is 5 adults to 1 child, not the other way around. Having more adults involved in your children's lives is very important. Children need guidance about what is happening in their world and as they learn about their purpose and mission. Developing their own relationship with God is also important, and mentorships can help them do that. There are many times when children, especially teens, don't want to talk to their parents. If they have other adults they can go to, it can be very helpful.

One of my teens struggled with the evolution-versus-creationism debate. What made the biggest impact for him as he wrestled through this aspect of faith was the leader of a Bible study he attended each week; the leader was a scientific researcher with a Ph.D. in cellular biology. Thus, my son could ask a person with an extensive scientific background about some of his doubts related to that aspect of faith.

When we were going through a tough time with another teenage son, I asked around and got the name of a young adult in our church who would be a good mentor. We contacted him, and he went out of his way to give my son a call once a week to chat and keep in touch with him. We really needed an outside person to be guiding and supporting our son when our relationship with him was strained.

Our children have been able to develop inter-generational relationships as a result of attending worship services with us. When we lived in Tucson, our home was near a retirement community. We went to the 8:00 a.m. service at our church, as did many members of that community, so most of the time Josh and Ben were the only children who went up for the children's sermon. To describe Josh as an extroverted child would be an understatement, and the entire congregation couldn't wait to see what the boys would say each week. There were lots of laughs from the congregation, and a lot of growth for the boys. Being in the service created an opportunity for my children to develop relationships with the elderly people in our congregation, which was a blessing to both parties. Because these relationships were developed, we visited one couple who were having some health challenges. When my boys got to "ride" their electric lift chair in their living room, the giggles of my boys and this couple were infectious!

When Josh was eight, our pastor took another call. At his farewell gathering, he said, "Invite me to Josh's ordination." God had taken hold of Josh's heart when he was very young, and I know those relationships made a difference. Over the years, I have kept in contact with several of these retired people at Christmas. Even though we moved away from Arizona 15 years ago, these friends still talk about how much they loved seeing the boys each week.

Listen and Allow Children to Question and Grow

As our children move into their late teen and young adult years, it is no longer *our* faith that sustains them. They will wrestle, discover, and decide to embrace (or reject) Christianity for themselves. As they are changing and challenging their beliefs, remember that the way you live out your faith has a greater impact on your child than any other factor; it is caught, not taught. Remember, too, that it is normal and okay for them to question—even disagree—as they try to figure this out on their own. Continue to foster your relationship with your child, rely on God through prayer and petition, and surround yourself with support from fellow Christians. Don't shoot your child's questions down and belittle them, but provide an environment for her to talk with you and dialogue about her thoughts and struggles. The youth group can also be a great place for a teen to ask questions, assuming it aligns with your own beliefs and the Word of God.

When I asked my son what his advice to parents would be on the topic of spirituality, he said, "Don't assume we know or understand." Create an environment where kids can ask tough questions or voice thoughts that contradict your own beliefs without inciting anger, belittlement, or scorn. Teens are trying to figure out their own beliefs with a lot of non-Christian influences around them. They are on a faith *journey*, just like you are, so build bridges, not walls. Our kids need to be able to dialogue and figure this out for themselves with the guidance and support of their family.

Prayer

Pray for and with your children every day. Place your kids at Jesus' feet and ask him to help them build a life-long faith. This is much easier said than done. Life gets busy, and I have often fallen short on praying for my kids. But when this happens, I regroup and make it a priority again. It is when I start my day in prayer that I find more peace in my day. Encourage your kids to do the same.

I find that young children love to pray, and it can be an important part of instilling a habit of gratefulness. The children can pray for what they are thankful for, pray for others, and pray how they want God to guide and help them in some personal struggle. This will instill gratitude, empathy, and belief in purpose for their life and a living God who cares about them and wants to help them.

Here are some of the resources and activities we have enjoyed over the years to teach kids about God or foster discussion about various aspects of faith.

- Christian music or radio
- Children's Bibles
- Bible
- Devotionals
- Missionary Stories
- *Veggie Tales DVDs*
- *What's in the Bible?*
- Scripture memory CDs

Audio dramas or books that address issues connected to faith like Focus on the Family's Radio Theaters:

- *The Chronicles of Narnia*
- *The Secret Garden*
- *Les Miserables.*

As we listen, I frequently stop the CD and ask the kids questions or talk with them about what is happening. For example, during *The Lion the Witch and the Wardrobe*, we discuss how Aslan is like God, how his death and resurrection mirror Jesus' sacrifice for us, how Edmund and Lucy and the others represent believers at different places in their faith life, and so on. (You can find even more recommendations at www. parentingsensibly.com.)

Keep reminders around your home as well. Have verses on the refrigerator, by your computer, or on your walls. You can write verses on your children's mirrors or windows with washable markers. These provide great reminders throughout the day for everyone. Go through daily devotional books together—many are designed so all ages can glean something from them.

God loves us and our kids unconditionally, and we must show that same love to our children. They must hear and know that we love *them*, not what they do or don't do. When kids make mistakes, it's common for people around them—including parents—to pull away or send them away. However, it's at those very moments that it is important to do the opposite: Pull your children close, and help them regain their identity in your family and as a child of God. Restoration often occurs through relationship.

Share your life and faith journeys with your children, and be sure to stop and listen to your kids. Don't lecture; listen more and help them feel that unconditional love. Show that God is a part of your everyday life, not just on Sundays.

1. Think about your own spiritual faith and what it means to you. How can you best teach and model this faith so your children understand what it means to them?
2. How can you show unconditional love and engage other safe mentors for your children to learn from?
3. Pray for your children and for your guidance as a parent.

Children's picture books that show unconditional love:
The Way Mothers Are by Miriam Schlein
The Runaway Bunny by Margaret Wise Brown

Book resources about praying for your family:
Praying God's Will for My Daughter by Lee Roberts
Praying God's Will for My Son by Lee Roberts
The Power of a Praying Parent by Stormie Ormartian

CHAPTER 17

Empowering Your Child
to Move Mountains

 PARENTING POINT: Make sure your children hear you say (directly or indirectly), "I love you and believe that you can accomplish the goals you set for yourself."

G rowing up, what I most dreaded about school was going to my physical education classes. In the 1970s, that class consisted of a rotation of many competitive sports. Usually the top two athletes in the class got to be team captains, and they chose teams one by one. I was always the last one standing; I was placed on a team by default, not because a leader chose me. When the games would start, I would try to position myself in the place on the field where I was least likely to see action.

My academic classes didn't feel much better. For many years, I couldn't say the letter R. It took weekly sessions with a speech pathologist in the third grade before I could enunciate my Rs—and by then, I had endured many years of teasing and laughter. My grades themselves were okay; I wasn't at the top, but I wasn't at the bottom. Comments on my report cards usually said things like, "Real pleasure to have in class," or "Demonstrates cooperation and courtesy." I was never in the top group; nothing made me stand out from the crowd.

I was sick for a good part of fifth grade. Sixth grade was a year I wish I could forget. A person who had been a friend since kindergarten started bullying me and somehow got the whole class to tease me the entire year. My books were regularly pushed off my desk; I was often scared at recess because kids would surround and taunt me. I felt alone and dejected.

Junior high wasn't any better. I was thankful that I had a kind homeroom teacher—and a bathroom across the hall—because every morning, my GI system would act up. One scrawny boy mercilessly teased me for having a flat chest, as I was an extremely late bloomer. However, by the end of eighth grade, I had made a few good friends, which was a great blessing for that time of my life.

In ninth grade, there was a fire in our house. My mom had put my gym clothes in the dryer while I was at a youth group event in a neighboring town. That evening, only my dad and little brother were home when a fire started because of lint in the dryer. By the time the smoke alarms went off on the main floor, the fire in the basement had burned the phone line, and the house quickly filled with smoke. When I arrived home that night, all our cars were parked away from the house and not one light was on. My dad came over from the neighbor's house as I was getting out of the car to explain about the fire, stating that we couldn't sleep in our own house for awhile.

The next day, I showed up to P.E. without my gym uniform. My gym teacher would not let me wear other shorts; instead, she made me wear an old one-piece striped gym uniform from many years prior. She told me that having my gym clothes burned in our house fire was not a good enough excuse. It was the start of some very tough months in the aftermath of the fire, and it was during that time that my dad told me, "I wish you had never been born."

I share all of this because I know how important the love and support of a parent, of a friend, of a teacher is—and how devastating it can be when you don't have it. Everyone needs to feel accepted, valued, and loved. This love and support is a feeling; and that feeling encompasses more than someone saying "I love you" once in a while. It comprises a sense of belonging, purpose, meaning, and value. This is what many people call feeling "the blessing" or not.

What do I mean by "blessing?" The Hebrew word for blessing is *Bracka* and is used over 640 times in the Old Testament. According to Merriam-Webster, one definition is approval or encouragement.[118] Blessing can also mean, "May God be with you." Sometimes you hear the term blessing used to describe a prayer said before a meal. Blessings are often given at a wedding, a baptism, an infant dedication, or some other ceremony.

What does this have to do with parenting? Whether we understand it in terms of blessing or not, we either have a feeling of parental acceptance and love or we do not. I highly recommend reading *The Blessing*,[119] by Gary Smalley and John Trent, for a much deeper understanding of this topic. It was instrumental for me years ago when I was processing my past hurts, and it gave me a foundation for passing on the blessing to my children. The framework and concepts for this chapter come from their book and my personal experiences. I will touch upon how we can be intentional in our parenting so that our children will feel this unconditional love and trust that we believe in a great future for them.

When the Blessing is Not Given

One biblical blessing story is the story of Esau and Jacob. They were twins, but Esau was the firstborn and so, by birthright, he should have received the blessing meant for the oldest son. But this family was riddled with favoritism: The twins' father Isaac loved Esau, and their mother Rebekah loved Jacob. Not only that, but there was tremendous rivalry between the two brothers. At one point, Esau "sold" his birthright to Jacob. Later, when Isaac was old, weak, and blind, Rebekah helped Jacob deceive Isaac so that the blessing was given to Jacob instead of Esau. In anguish, Esau cried out and wept over his lost blessing (Genesis 27:36-38).

How many people weep just like Esau, wanting so much to have their parent's blessing and approval? Homes where favoritism reigns leave many children feeling worthless. Other homes have abusive and controlling parents, neglectful parents, or manipulative parents who have significantly wounded their children instead of giving them their blessing. Some of those children grow up to become workaholics, thinking things like, "If I just gain the next level of success, maybe then my parent will say, 'Good job! I am so proud of you.'" Some people become angry and bitter, while others cover up the pain through addictions. Some become depressed and withdrawn, and others try to find that blessing through things, thinking that they will find fulfillment if they just buy this car, that house, or other items. In families with divorce, desertion, or the death of a parent, children may never receive the blessing from a parent and may grow up blaming themselves for its lack.

There are so many homes where a parent's blessing is not given to a child, and we have a huge number of broken people struggling through life as a result. Whatever the root cause for these feelings of rejection, there is good news: There can be healing and restoration of this blessing. I know, because I have felt this myself.

If you had a healthy parent/child relationship and felt this blessing from your parents, please be sure to follow their example and pass that onto your children. To bless your children is to say, "I value you greatly, and I want to add to your life." But for those of us who have not been so fortunate, here are a few ideas that can help you break the cycle and provide that blessing your children need from you.

The five elements of the blessing:

1. Meaningful and appropriate touch
2. A spoken message
3. Attaching high value to the one being blessed
4. Picturing a special future for him or her
5. An active commitment to fulfill the blessing

(Taken from *The Blessing: Giving the Gift of Unconditional Love and Acceptance* by John Trent and Gary Smalley, Copyright 1986, 1993, 2011 John Trent and Gary Smalley. Used by permission by Thomas Nelson. www.thomasnelson.com)

1. Meaningful and Appropriate Touch

Touch is an important part of giving the blessing. How important? When I worked as a pediatric nurse, the unit next to mine was a general pediatric unit, where many infants who were admitted had "failure to thrive"—that is, they were not gaining adequate weight at home. Many medical problems can prevent a child from gaining weight; one of them, which may be surprising to some, is a lack of bonding between the parent and child. That doesn't necessarily mean a parent isn't feeding the child or providing some sort of care; rather, in spite of giving surface-level care, some of those parents are detached. In the cases I saw while working as a nurse, often the parents of these infants would not look at or hold their children; instead, they would do things like prop the bottle so that the baby could feed in an infant carrier while they watched TV. To help these children survive, doctors had to teach the parents to engage with and touch their children. This is also true for older children; children and teens also struggle in homes where there is parental neglect or abuse.

When I was a nursing student, I witnessed the power of touch in a child's life firsthand. As part of my training, I spent a couple of weeks at a residential facility for severely disabled children, where I cared for an 8-year-old who had severe brain trauma from having meningitis as an infant. She could not move, sit by herself, walk, or talk. She had an 8-year-old body, but beyond opening her eyes, there was not much she could do to communicate, and I had a difficult time connecting with her. Finally, I sat with her in my lap, rocking her gently and singing. Her body, which until that point had been rigid, relaxed in my arms, and I could literally feel that I was connecting with her. Touch was the key to communicating with this child.

We can offer meaningful appropriate physical touch to our children through things like hugs, kisses, tossing them in the air, giving them piggyback rides, holding them on our laps as we read to them, offering back rubs, and holding hands when walking. As children grow older, they may respond better to high-fives, playful wrestling, bear hugs, manicures and pedicures, or shoulder massages. It is so important for this need for touch to be filled at home so that our kids do not seek it elsewhere. There have been many studies that support the impact of touch on both physical and emotional well-being. (See Chapter 4 for more about how touch is an effective love language.)

2. Spoken Words

The words we speak are powerful. Thus, we must be very attentive to what we say. We are like a mirror: when we say things about our children, that becomes how our children see themselves. Our words also reveal what is in our heart; circumstances may cause us to say things we would normally hold back, but that doesn't change the fact that we say what is already on our hearts and minds.[120] We need to fix our own attitudes.

The Bible is filled with wisdom about how to watch our words. Ephesians 4:29 instructs us to use words that encourage and build people up. This sums up perfectly the power of our words as we give (or don't give) our children our blessing. Are we choosing words that build our children up according to their needs? Our job is to study our children and help guide them toward becoming who God created them to be. Proverbs 15:1 (NIV) says, "A gentle answer turns away wrath, but a harsh word stirs up anger." As parents, we know (or should be striving to learn) what tips our children over the edge. Instead of doing that, we must work on using gentle and encouraging words.

The opposite of speaking a blessing is speaking a curse. I'm not referring to bad language (though certainly that can be part of it); rather, I'm referring to how we describe and define our children. We don't want to label kids as a "slow learner," "sickly child," "difficult," or "hyperactive." We need to have faith that God will work through all situations with our children, and instead make sure to focus on speaking positives into our children.

Be careful to avoid demeaning or harsh accusations like, "Can't you do anything right?" If a child wants to try something, don't say things like, "Don't waste your time with try-outs; you're never going to get a part anyway." After the death of a pet, don't say, "What are you crying about? It was just a dog."

Beyond harsh and negative words, though, we must also watch what we say with positive intentions, too—don't say you are going to do something and then make some excuse to not follow through. Watch your words, tone, and body language when angry. Silence can also be harmful, as our children seek and need to hear approval. Remember, we are the mirrors that show our children their worth to us.

At the start of this chapter, I shared with you some of my painful childhood moments. By far, the most painful of those moments was when my father said, "I wish you would have never been born." Those words ate me up. He said them in anger after he had been drinking, stressed about our financial situation because of the fire. He never remembered saying them, but they could not be taken back, and they played in my head for many, many years. Those words showed I had no worth or value. I started doing things I probably wouldn't have done. I had a strong need to belong and found that belonging meant being in the party crowd. I got depressed and made poor relationship choices. Eventually, my relationship with my father was restored (as I will explain soon), but there is no denying the impact those words have had on my life.

3. Expressing High Value and Importance

Think back to your childhood, to those moments where you felt most valued. What were the things that were said or done that made you feel valued? Did that feeling of value and importance come only at certain moments, or was it something you constantly felt—even if you weren't doing anything particularly noteworthy?

There are many ways we can express to our children just how much we value them, and it should not just happen when they've made an achievement. When children receive praise only when they perform, they feel that their parents' love is conditional—it only comes when they do something special. So, we need to work to make sure our children recognize our love for them is true and unconditional, no matter what they have or have not been doing. Your words can give value, hope, and encouragement.

4. Envisioning a Child's Special Future

When we feel hopeful about the future, we can cope much better through difficult times. When you look back into your childhood, you may remember positive or negative comments about your future. You may have fulfilled those or been successful despite them.

As I mentioned earlier in the chapter, I was an average student. When I was in second grade, our class was too big, so we had to be divided into two classrooms. From my understanding, the smart kids went in the other class; I was not part of that group, and so I thought I was not smart. This view of myself affected me greatly all through high school and into college. It wasn't until I was a junior in college, when I did a lot of introspection, that I realized I was just as smart as any of the other girls in my nursing class. After that, my grades showed a significant improvement—my changed attitude about my abilities allowed me to reach a greater potential. It's amazing how those small things that cause us to have such a negative view of our talents can have such a lasting impact—and vice versa.

To look at it from another angle, think of that person who encouraged you in something growing up—maybe it was academic skills in music, art, reading, or math. Perhaps it was in practical skills, like complimenting your skills as a babysitter, or remarking on your talent at building something. Do you remember working extra hard at that task after someone encouraged you? These words of genuine encouragement—not just empty flattery—encourage us to continue developing those skills.

Thus, our goal in envisioning a special future for our children is to create a positive, hopeful attitude that encourages our children so that they can build their confidence and accomplish their dreams. The phrase, "To train a child in the way he should go" (Proverbs 22.6 KJV), does *not* say "the way we want them to go." Instead, it refers to our task to help our children find their own unique path. If a child shows an interest in being a fireman, a teacher, or a ballet dancer, don't discourage them, but encourage them to pursue their passions.

By envisioning a special future for her daughter, Temple Grandin's mother opened doors that would otherwise have been closed. Temple has Asperger's, a disorder on the autistic spectrum. In the 1950s, very little was understood about the disorder, and experts insisted that Temple be institutionalized. But her mother was an incredible example of speaking the blessing to her daughter. Temple didn't speak until she was four, and so her mother brought her from school to school to find someone who would educate her. Her mother accepted that yes, Temple was different, but she was *not less* than any other child. She saw in her daughter a potential that no one else did. Eventually, Temple *did* do great things, one of which still has a tremendous impact in the meat industry on the process of slaughtering cattle for food; more than half the industry uses her system today. She is also an author and public speaker; I highly recommend watching or listening to her TED talk, "The World Needs all Kinds of Minds."[121] When the experts of the time didn't have any hope for her future, her mother did, and Temple's accomplishments were great.

Just as Temple's mother actively showed her support, your child needs to know that you support and believe in him or her.

5. An Active Commitment

It is one thing to speak about your child's special future, but the next step of active commitment needs to be taken to make this future a reality. Our words of encouragement and high value don't mean anything if we don't make an active commitment to help our children reach their goals. If our child dreams of being a concert pianist, and we tell him he is very talented and could become that pianist, but we don't provide him with piano lessons, the words are meaningless.

When my son became interested in graphic design, we had him call my brother, who is a graphic designer, to chat about what he would recommend learning. My brother encouraged my son to learn how to use Adobe Photoshop because it was the main platform in the industry and would be extremely useful. So Dave and I invested in that program, and then we incorporated learning Photoshop tutorials into our son's coursework. Study your child, open doors, provide the lessons and supplies as you are able, and seek mentors who can provide both additional training and encouragement for your child as they pursue that passion.

Never Too Late for Change

As we look at these elements of passing on our blessing to our children, it can be discouraging to see areas where we have failed. If our children are older, we may also wonder if we might be too little, too late in changing our behaviors and communicating how much we love and value them. But as my own story shows, it's never too late for those moments of reconciliation.

I said earlier that I spent years ruminating over my father's words and made a lot of poor choices out of the resulting sense of worthlessness and despair I felt. But it wasn't until the summer after my sophomore year of college that my father became aware of this.

On the day I was leaving to go back for my third year of college classes, my dad and I took the dog for a walk. I was angry at my dad, and I had been for many years, because of those words. He asked what I was so angry about, so I finally told him. He was speechless. He had no idea.

You see, a few years before this fateful walk, my parents had gone through a bankruptcy and lost everything. They moved to Arizona to start over. In a new state, a new town, with no material wealth and no friends, my mom and dad began a new stage of life—no drinking buddies; no poker nights. Just Mom and Dad, spending time together. As a result, their relationship—and their lives—started to change for the better. The father I walked with that day was a different man than the one who, years before, had told me that he wished I'd never been born.

And so, having now realized what had caused a years-long wedge in our relationship, my dad wrote me a letter. He explained that although he had no recollection of this conversation, he was sorry for what he had said and done. Though I can no longer find the letter, its words impacted me deeply (and continue to do so today).

Over the next several years, I started to soften toward my dad. He was changing as well. After Dave and I married and finished our studies, we moved to Arizona to start his first career job. We lived with my parents for a few months while we were house hunting, and then they moved in with us for six months while they were building a new house.

Things were by no means perfect. In those years, when we had our first children, my parents had parenting advice for me that I was not receptive to because of my resentment around my own childhood. But it was during this time that I started to understand why my dad had parented the way he did—how his own childhood had impacted how he had raised me. He didn't know how to show love because he hadn't experienced it. He doesn't remember ever being told he was loved by his parents.

This shows how important the blessing is in a family's story. When the blessing is withheld, this same pattern can go on for generations. Even though there exist abusive or very dysfunctional families where restoration with parents may not be possible, it is still helpful to understand those parents' backgrounds, to comprehend why they did what they did, and to learn how to break that cycle for your children through everyday parenting choices.

I realized I had to show grace to my father, and that I had to forgive. It was a decision that I made; not a feeling I suddenly had. Our parents are imperfect, just as we are. I hope my children will one day forgive me for all the things I have screwed up over the years, and my parents deserve the same forgiveness.

Forgiveness isn't about saying that what misguided parents did was right, but it is about releasing those wrongs from your own burden. In Matthew 6:14-15, Jesus tells us that in order to be forgiven, we must also forgive. I started to soften; I learned how to let go of more and more of my anger and not react as badly to genuine offers of advice and love from my dad. I realized how important it was to let go of that toxic anger; it was important for me to stop the blame game and release that anger. I realized that, just as we long for the blessing from our parents, so do our parents long for that blessing of love from us. I was able to start looking at what my parents had done right and start expressing love and forgiveness to them. Once I could forgive—truly forgive—peace could be restored between my parents and me.

It was also about this time that my dad moved to South Carolina to sell homes there. My mom had to stay behind to sell their house and finish her teaching contract. Three fellow salesmen at his office asked my father to join them in prayer before work, and they became strong mentors in his walk with Christ. He has been involved in intense Bible study since that time.

When my mother moved out to join him in South Carolina, she met a new, changed husband. It was some time after this that he looked at the couple of beers he still drank every day and said, "No more." He vowed to never touch alcohol again, and he never has. He started praying for an hour a day. He prayed for *me* every day! He became a source of encouragement, and his anger, which had been steadily decreasing since that first move to Arizona, was gone. I am so thankful for God's work in this situation; as it says in Romans 8:28 (NIV), "And we know that in all things God works for the good of those who love him, who have been called according to his purpose."

As awful as going through the bankruptcy was, in hindsight, it saved my father and our family. He was a new person in Christ, just as it says in 2 Corinthians 5:17 (NIV): "Therefore, if anyone is in Christ, the new creation has come: The old has gone, the new is here!" We had attended church my whole life—and my father had been a church-goer for about 30 years—but it was when the knowledge went to his heart and his relationship with Jesus truly began that miraculous changes happened. This happened 23 years ago. My children only know my father as this changed person. My father recently said he never felt love until he felt the love of Christ.

This does not mean, however, that it has always been easy between my father and me. About six years ago, my parents were visiting for an extended period of time. At the time, our home group was doing a book study on Philip Yancey's *What's So Amazing About Grace?*[122] It is a fabulous book and has many examples of cases in which it would seem *impossible* to forgive: rape, murder, enduring the Holocaust, and more. (If you are struggling to forgive, please read this book.) My parents came each week to the study. Off and on during those weeks, my dad would bring up various issues that he was seeing with my kids. I took it as judgment, and I started harboring some resentment—after all, I thought, who was *he* to tell me how to parent?

At one point, he was talking about preventing sibling rivalry between a few of my kids, and I said, "Like all those times you helped me out when my older brother was picking on me?" I told him about many of my childhood moments—how I was humiliated in front of other children. I was picked on constantly. I shared how my cousin, who was my age, wouldn't play with me, because she was afraid she would be a target for being picked on, too. My dad was silent. He had no idea. How would he? He was not around much and when he was, he was asleep on the chair in front of the T.V. He wasn't an active presence at that point in my life.

That was just one of the tough moments we had in that time. By the end of the three-week visit, I was agitated by the childhood memories that had surfaced. I didn't know whether to confront my dad or just let it be. It was the past. I had forgiven, hadn't I? I decided the night before my parents left to let it be.

Early the next morning, however, I went downstairs to get some dinner things out of the freezer. In that house, I had to go through the guest bedroom to get to our storage room where the freezer was. My dad stopped me and said he wanted to talk to me; he had been waiting for a moment when I was alone. He said, "I just wanted to let you know that I am sorry. I am sorry for the hurts I caused you when you were growing up." That is all that was said. We hugged and wept.

Some of you will never get that opportunity for reconciliation. But the beautiful thing is that even if you don't receive that blessing from your earthly fathers or mothers, our heavenly Father gives you his blessing. It is unconditional. He loves *you*! He forgives *you*. He wants to have a relationship with *you*! This is not based on anything you have or have not done. God's blessing is irrevocable and his love is unconditional. Read Psalm 23 to see how God feels about you!

I highly recommend reading the picture book *You are Special*,[123] by Max Lucado, to your children. It is a beautiful story relating God's unconditional love. It is an excellent book any time, but I find that it is particularly helpful on the days when a child had a rough day. Another great picture book on this topic is *I'd Choose You*,[124] by John Trent.

The last—and most important—point I want to make in this chapter is this: With the help of God we CAN break the cycle of withholding the blessing, and we can make sure the passing on of the blessing continues to the next generation. We can give our children the blessing—each of them, not just the oldest.

I want you all to sit down and write out a blessing for each of your children and your spouse if you have one. For a more in-depth description on how to do this, read *The Blessing: Giving the Gift of Unconditional Love and Acceptance* and go to Gary Smalley and John Trent's website: http://www.theblessing.com

Take time to think through the elements of the blessing and put into words how special each child is to you. By putting it in writing, they will hear, see, and have something they can read over and over again. Then use meaningful touch, positive spoken words, expressions of high value, your envisioning of a special future for your kids, and an active commitment to them throughout their lives. Empower your children to follow their dreams and passions and to work toward fulfilling God's plan for their lives. As parents, this is the most sensible thing we can do.

Numbers 6:24-26 NIV[125]
May the... "Lord bless you, and keep you:
the Lord make his face shine on you and be gracious to you:
the Lord turn his face toward you and give you peace."

1. For more information, go to: http://www. theblessing.com
2. Write out a blessing for each child.
3. Write down ways you can use components of the blessing throughout your days.

AFTERWORD

In a perfect world, everything would be smooth sailing from here on out; you would be able to translate every lesson you have learned into an action that is immediately successful in changing your family's life. But we all know life isn't like that, and neither is parenting; as always, it will continue to be filled with joy and challenges, laughter and tears—sometimes even in the same moment! However, now you have tools to better navigate through the ups and downs ahead.

We covered a lot of ground in this book. To help you remember everything, I've developed a quick-hits list to jog your memory of all the things you have learned:

- Your past affects you, but it does not determine your future.
- There is no perfect parent or child.
- Be attentive to personalities—both your child's and your own.
- Express love consistently and in a variety of ways; everyone gives and receives love best through different methods, so it is helpful to be able to be fluent in all of them.
- Remember the 4 Cs:
  - Communication: Make sure you communicate clearly with your kids.
  - Coaching: Train your child, making sure they have room to practice and learn, as well as to come to you with questions if they forget or don't understand something.

- ° Consequences: Allow your child to experience life's lessons through both successes and failures, as this is the best way to learn.
- ° Connection: When there is disobedience or other negative behavior, reconciliation is an important step to maintaining a healthy connection with your child.
- Respond; don't react.
- Happiness is a choice.
- Encourage effort.
- Major on the majors, minor on the minors: Pick which things are important to address.
- How we parent today is laying the foundation for who our children will be in 20 years.
- Try to eat at home together as often as you can.
- Be a family that serves others.
- Everyone is part of the family, so everyone pitches in to help.
- Don't do for your children what they can do for themselves.
- Keep an attitude of gratitude in your home.
- Teach solid financial principles, and allow your child more and more opportunities to make financial decisions as he or she gets older. Encourage and enable your child to earn money instead of always receiving it without effort on their part.
- Give your child a firm spiritual foundation and set a good example.
- Pray often.
- Express worth and value to your child. We are mirrors, reflecting how our children see themselves.

These are all helpful tips, but I know as well as anyone that even with these lessons, one reality won't change: Parenting is hard. Don't give up; remain steadfast on this parenting journey. You have read this book, so I know that you take parenting seriously and want to do the best job you can. That alone makes a tremendous difference in your parenting. *Keep loving your children unconditionally and continue believing in them.* In addition, *encourage effort, passion, problem-solving, and strong work ethic. Start looking at your child with a different lens. Encourage effort, not achievements. Address mistakes and challenges as opportunities for learning, not failures. Turn those messes into successes!*

You can do this, one sensible step at a time!

And please, I encourage you—stay connected with me! My website (www.parentingsensibly.com) has numerous additional articles, topics, and many more resources that you can use every day in your parenting.

ENDNOTES

1. The Mom's Class was taught by Barbara Tompkins at The Journey Church in Tucson, AZ.
2. Diana Baumrind, "Effects of Authoritative Parental Control on Child Behavior," Child Development 37(1966):887-907
3. West, Matthew, The Story of Your Life, "Family Tree" Sparrow Records, 2010, compact disc
4. "Breastfeeding Mum's Meal Cut up by a Lady in a Cafe - Kidspot." 2017. Accessed August 7. http://www.kidspot.com.au/baby/feeding/breastfeeding/ we-are-melting-over-the-sweet-thing-a-woman-did-for-a-breastfeeding-mum/ news-story/718ca333ac12e7817b3361e4eae1f389?
5. Smalley, Gary, and John Trent. *The Two Sides of Love.* Colorado Springs: Focus on the Family, Carol Stream: Tyndale House Publishers, Inc., 1992.
6. Ibid.
7. Ibid.
8. Boyd, Charles F., and Robert A. Rohm. 2004. *Different Children, Different Needs.* Rev. ed. Sisters, Or: Multnomah.
9. Gregston, Mark. 2008. *Dealing with Today's Teens: A Seminar for Parents and Youth Workers Workbook.* Hallsville, TX: Heartlight Ministries Foundation.
10. Chapman, Gary. 2015. *The 5 Love Languages: The Secret to Love That Lasts.* 1st edition. Chicago: Northfield Publishing.
11. Chapman, Gary D., and Ross Campbell. 2016. *The 5 Love Languages of Children: The Secret to Loving Children Effectively.* Reissue edition. Chicago: Northfield Publishing.
12. Chapman, Gary D. 2016. *The 5 Love Languages of Teenagers: The Secret to Loving Teens Effectively.* Reissue edition. Chicago: Northfield Publishing.
13. Varela-Silva, Inês. 2017. "Can a Lack of Love Be Deadly?" *The Conversation.* Accessed June 8. http://theconversation.com/can-a-lack-of-love-be-deadly-58659.

14. Gregston, Mark. 2008. *Dealing with Today's Teens: A Seminar for Parents and Youth Workers Workbook*. Hallsville, TX: Heartlight Ministries Foundation.

15. Chase, Betty N. 1982. *Discipline Them, Love Them: Practical Projects for Parents*. Elgin, Ill.: David C. Cook.

16. The Moms Class was taught by Barbara Tompkins at The Journey Church in Tucson, Arizona.

17. Ibid.

18. "Definition of DISCIPLINE." 2017. Accessed May 19. https://www.merriam-webster.com/dictionary/discipline.

19. "Definition of PUNISHMENT." 2017. Accessed May 19. https://www.merriam-webster.com/dictionary/punishment.

20. The Moms Class was taught by Barbara Tompkins at The Journey Church in Tucson, Arizona.

21. "Ages & Stages." 2017. *HealthyChildren.org*. Accessed July 13. http://www.healthychildren.org/english/ages-stages/pages/default.aspx.

22. Zolotow, Charlotte. 1963. *The Quarreling Book*. New York, NY: Harper Collins Publishers.

23. The Moms Class was taught by Barbara Tompkins at The Journey Church in Tucson, Arizona.

24. "Attitudes." Copyright © 1981, 1982, by Charles R. Swindoll, Inc. All rights are reserved worldwide. Used by permission. www.insight.org

25. Leman, Kevin. 2008. *Have a New Kid by Friday*. Grand Rapids, MI: Revell.

26. Chase, Betty N. 1982. *Discipline Them, Love Them: Practical Projects for Parents*. Elgin, Ill.: David C. Cook.

27. The Moms Class was taught by Barbara Tompkins at The Journey Church in Tucson, Arizona.

28. Chase, Betty N. 1982. *Discipline Them, Love Them: Practical Projects for Parents*. Elgin, Ill.: David C. Cook.

29. Gilmer, Marcus. 2016. "Boy Abandoned in Forest by Parents as Punishment Found Six Days Later." *Mashable.com*, June 2. http://mashable.com/2016/06/02/japanese-boy-found/#7s5yvCRx7aqL

30. "Parenting Styles: A Guide for the Science-Minded." 2017. Accessed May 11. http://www.parentingscience.com/parenting-styles.html.

31. Baumrind, Diana. 1966. "Effects of Authoritative Parental Control on Child Behavior." *Child Development* 37(4): 887–907.

32. Elmore, Tim. 2013. "What Parents Should Say as Their Kids Perform." *Growing Leaders*. August 16. https://growingleaders.com/blog/what-parents-should-say-as-their-kids-perform/.

33. Grant, Adam. 2014. "Raising a Moral Child." *New York Times*, April 11. https://www.nytimes.com/2014/04/12/opinion/sunday/raising-a-moral-child.html?_r=1.

34. Smalley, Gary. 1992. *The Key to Your Child's Heart.* Nashville: Thomas Nelson.

35. Kemp, Jeff. 2012. "Performance Vs. Relationship Based Love." *Jeff Kemp Team.* January 31. http://www.jeffkempteam.com/performance-vs-relationship-based-love-2/.

36. Vivinetto, Gina. 2016. "Mom and Daughter Exchange Hilarious Texts over 'Drugs' Misunderstanding." *Today.* June 9. http://www.today.com/news/mom-daughter-exchange-hilarious-texts-over-drugs-misunderstanding-t97271.

37. Lynn, Jonathan. 1992. *My Cousin Vinny.* Comedy, Drama.

38. "The Power of a Smile - How Smiling Can Change Your Life and Change the World." 2012. *The Start of Happiness.* September 17. http://www.startofhappiness.com/the-power-of-a-smile/.

39. Chase, Betty N. 1982. *Discipline Them, Love Them: Practical Projects for Parents.* Elgin, Ill.: David C. Cook.

40. Moody, Ralph. 1991. Copyright 1950 by Ralph Moody. Copyright renewed 1978 by Ralph Moody. *Little Britches: Father and I Were Ranchers.* Lincoln: University of Nebraska Press.

41. "Declining Student Resilience: A Serious Problem for Colleges." 2017. *Psychology Today.* Accessed June 12. https://www.psychologytoday.com/blog/freedom-learn/201509/declining-student-resilience-serious-problem-colleges.

42. Chase, Betty N, Dave Jackson, and Neta Jackson. 1982. *Discipline Them, Love Them: Practical Projects for Parents.* Elgin, Ill.: David C. Cook.

43. Ibid.

44. The Moms Class was taught by Barbara Tompkins at The Journey Church in Tucson, AZ.

45. Leman, Kevin. 2012. *Have a New Kid by Friday: How to Change Your Child's Attitude, Behavior & Character in 5 Days.* Reprint edition. Revell.

46. "Rewards and Praise: The Poisoned Carrot - The Natural Child Project." 2017. Accessed July 14. http://www.naturalchild.org/robin_grille/rewards_praise.html.

47. Fawson, Parker C., and Sharon A. Moore. 1999. "Reading Incentive Programs: Beliefs and Practices." *Reading Psychology* 20 (4): 325–40.

48. "Alfie Kohn on Oprah." 1996. *Rewards.*

49. Kohn, Alfie. 1999. *Punished by Rewards: The Trouble with Gold Stars, Incentive Plans, A's, Praise, and Other Bribes.* Boston: Houghton Mifflin Co.

50. Chase, Betty N, Dave Jackson, and Neta Jackson. 1982. *Discipline Them, Love Them: Practical Projects for Parents.* Elgin, Ill.: David C. Cook.

51. Pink, Dan. 2009. *The Puzzle of Motivation.* Ted Talk. Accessed May 10. https://www.ted.com/talks/dan_pink_on_motivation.

52. Kohn, Alfie. 1999. *Punished by Rewards: The Trouble with Gold Stars, Incentive Plans, A's, Praise, and Other Bribes.* Boston: Houghton Mifflin Co.

53. Stanfield, Gayle M. (2008) "Incentives: The Effects on Reading Attitude and Reading Behaviors of Third-Grade Students," The Corinthian: Vol. 9, Article 8. Available at: http://kb.gcsu.edu/thecorinthian/vol9/iss1/8

54. *Cierra Runge-USA Swimming Olympic Team 2016*. 2016. USA Swimming Oympic Team 2016. https://www.youtube.com/watch?v=XZhK5PFyqR0.

55. Schwartz, Barry. 2007. "Money for Nothing." *New York Times*, July 2. http://www.nytimes.com/2007/07/02/opinion/02schwartz.html.

56. Gneezy, Uri, and Aldo Rustichini. 2000. "A Fine Is a Price." *Journal of Legal Studies* XXIX (January). http://rady.ucsd.edu/faculty/directory/gneezy/pub/docs/fine.pdf.

57. Zhao, Y., and Encinosa, W. Hospitalizations for Eating Disorders from 1999 to 2006. HCUP Statistical Brief #70. April 2009. Agency for Healthcare Research and Quality, Rockville, MD. http://www.hcupus.ahrq.gov/reports/statbriefs/sb70.pdf.

58. "AbigailNatenshon.com - When Young Children Have Eating Disorders." 2017. Accessed July 15. https://treatingeatingdisorders.com/youngchildren.aspx.

59. Bronson, Po. 2007. "How Not to Talk to Your Kids: The Inverse Power of Praise." *New York Magazine*, August 3. http://nymag.com/news/features/27840/.

60. Lepper, Mark, and David Greene. 1973. "Undermining Children's Intrinsic Interest with Extrinsic Reward: A Test of the 'Overjustification' Hypothesis." *Journal of Personality and Social Psychology* 28 (1): 129–37.

61. "Opie's Ill-Gotten Gain." 1963. *Andy Griffith Show*.

62. Delton, Judy, and Lillian Hoban. 1983. *I'm Telling You Now*. 1st ed. New York: E.P. Dutton.

63. Chase, Betty N., Dave Jackson, and Neta Jackson. 1982. *Discipline Them, Love Them: Practical Projects for Parents*. Elgin, Ill.: David C. Cook.

64. Rubin, Gretchen Craft. 2011. *The Happiness Project ; Or, Why I Spent a Year Trying to Sing in the Morning, Clean My Closets, Fight Right, Read Aristotle, and Generally Have More Fun*. New York: Harper.

65. Talwar, Victoria, Cindy Arruda, and Sarah Yachison. 2015. "The Effects of Punishment and Appeals for Honesty on Children's Truth-Telling Behavior." *Journal of Experimental Child Psychology* 130 (February): 209–17. doi:10.1016/j.jecp.2014.09.011.

66. Friedman, Thomas. 2011. "How About Better Parents?" *New York Times*, November 19. http://www.nytimes.com/2011/11/20/opinion/sunday/friedman-how-about-better-parents.html.

67. Kindlon, Daniel J. 2001. *Too Much of a Good Thing: Raising Children of Character in an Indulgent Age*. 1st ed. New York: Hyperion.

68. Ibid.

69. The National Center on Addiction and Substance Abuse. (2012). *The importance of family dinners VIII.* New York: Califano, Joseph A.

70. Snow, Catherine E., and Diane E. Beals. 2006. "Mealtime Talk That Supports Literacy Development." *New Directions for Child and Adolescent Development* 2006 (111): 51–66. doi:10.1002/cd.155.

71. Cullen KW, Baranowski T. "Influence of family dinner on food intake of 4th to 6th grade students." *J Am Diet Assoc.* 2000:100(suppl): A38.

72. Wildavsky, R. "What's behind success in school?" Lou Harris-Reader's Digest national poll. Readers Digest Association, Pleasantville, NY; 1994.

73. Neumark-Sztainer, Dianne, Nicole I. Larson, Jayne A. Fulkerson, Marla E. Eisenberg, and Mary Story. 2010. "Family Meals and Adolescents: What Have We Learned from Project EAT (Eating Among Teens)?" *Public Health Nutrition* 13 (7): 1113–21. doi:10.1017/S1368980010000169.

74. *CBS NEWS.* 2015. "Many U.S. Kids Eat Fast Food Every Day," September 16. http://www.cbsnews.com/news/many-u-s-kids-eat-fast-food-every-day/.

75. Reinberg, Steven. 2012. "For Kids, Eating Out=More Calories." *U.S. News & World Report*, November 5. http://health.usnews.com/health-news/news/articles/2012/11/05/for-kids-eating-out--more-calories.

76. Imus, Deirdre. 2012. "Limit Fast Food Advertising toward Kids, Lower Childhood Obesity Rates." *Fox News*, July 20. http://www.foxnews.com/health/2012/07/20/stop-fast-food-advertising-lower-childhood-obesity-rates.html.

77. Neumark-Sztainer, Dianne, Nicole I. Larson, Jayne A. Fulkerson, Marla E. Eisenberg, and Mary Story. 2010. "Family Meals and Adolescents: What Have We Learned from Project EAT (Eating Among Teens)?" *Public Health Nutrition* 13 (7): 1113–21. doi:10.1017/S1368980010000169.

78. Eisenberg, Marla E., Rachel E. Olson, Dianne Neumark-Sztainer, Mary Story, and Linda H. Bearinger. 2004. "Correlations between Family Meals and Psychosocial Well-Being among Adolescents." *Archives of Pediatrics & Adolescent Medicine* 158 (8): 792–96. doi:10.1001/archpedi.158.8.792.

79. Zollo, Peter. 1999. *Wise Up to Teens: Insights into Marketing and Advertising to Teenagers.* 2nd edition. Ithaca, N.Y: New Strategist Pubns Inc.

80. Fruh, Sharon M., Jayne A. Fulkerson, Madhuri S. Mulekar, Lee Ann J. Kendrick, and Clista Clanton. 2011. "The Surprising Benefits of the Family Meal." *The Journal for Nurse Practitioners* 7 (1): 18–22. doi:10.1016/j.nurpra. 2010.04.017.

81. Scripture quotations marked (NIV) are taken from the Holy Bible, New International Version®, NIV®. Copyright © 1973, 1978, 1984, 2011 by Biblica, Inc.™ Used by permission of Zondervan. All rights reserved worldwide. www.zondervan.com The "NIV" and "New International Version" are trademarks registered in the United States Patent and Trademark Office by Biblica, Inc.™

82. Dahl, Roald. 2016. Ill. Blake, Quentin. *Charlie and the Chocolate Factory*. Reissue edition. Puffin Books.

83. Kindlon, Daniel J. 2001. *Too Much of a Good Thing: Raising Children of Character in an Indulgent Age*. 1st ed. New York: Hyperion.

84. Piliavin, Jane Allyn, and Erica Siegl. 2007. "Health Benefits of Volunteering in the Wisconsin Longitudinal Study." *Journal of Health and Social Behavior* 48 (4): 450–64. doi:10.1177/002214650704800408.

85. www.kiva.org

86. www.compassion.com

87. "Unintentional Drowning: Get the Facts." 2017. Centers for Disease Control and Prevention. Accessed May 10. https://www.cdc.gov/homeandrecreationalsafety/water-safety/waterinjuries-factsheet.html.

88. Kindlon, Daniel J. 2001. *Too Much of a Good Thing: Raising Children of Character in an Indulgent Age*. 1st ed. New York: Hyperion.

89. Rossmann, Marty. 2002. "Involving Children in Household Tasks: Is It Worth the Effort?" University of Minnesota. http://ghk.h-cdn.co/assets/cm/15/12/55071e0298a05_-_Involving-children-in-household-tasks-U-of-M.pdf.

90. Fry, Richard. 2016. "For First Time in Modern Era, Living With Parents Edges Out Other Living Arrangements for 18-34 Year Olds." *Pew Research Center*. May 24. http://www.pewsocialtrends.org/2016/05/24/for-first-time-in-modern-era-living-with-parents-edges-out-other-living-arrangements-for-18-to-34-year-olds/.

91. Covey, Stephen R. 2013. *The 7 Habits of Highly Effective People: Powerful Lessons in Personal Change*. 25th anniversary edition. New York: Simon & Schuster.

92. Stuart, Annie. 2012. "Divide and Conquer Household Chores." *WebMD*. December 2. http://www.webmd.com/parenting/features/chores-for-children#1.

93. *The Paradox of Choice*. 2017. Ted Talk. Accessed May 10. https://www.ted.com/talks/barry_schwartz_on_the_paradox_of_choice.

94. Barnes, Robert G. 1997. *Ready for Responsibility: How to Equip Your Children for Work and Marriage*. Grand Rapids, MI: Zondervan Publishing House.

95. Steindl-Rast, David, and Henri J. M. Nouwen. 1984. *Gratefulness, The Heart of Prayer: An Approach to Life in Fullness*. First Edition. New York: Paulist Press.

96. Leher, Jonah. 2010. "Why Money Makes You Unhappy." *Wired*, July 21. https://www.wired.com/2010/07/happiness-and-money-2/.

97. Millburn, Joshua, and Ryan Nicodemus. n.d. *The Minimalist Podcast*. The Minimalists. http://www.theminimalists.com/.

98. "Happiness, Wealth and the Amish." 2017. *The Frontal Cortex*. Accessed July 28. http://scienceblogs.com/cortex/2007/03/16/happiness-wealth-and-the-amish/.

99. Morin, Amy. 2015. "7 Scientifically Proven Benefits of Gratitude," April 3. https://www.psychologytoday.com/blog/what-mentally-strong-people-dont-do/201504/7-scientifically-proven-benefits-gratitude.

100. Emmons, Robert, and Michael McCullough. 2003. "Counting Blessings versus Burdens: An Experimental Investigation of Gratitude and Subjective Well-Being in Daily Life." *APA PsycNET American Psychological Association* 84 (2): 377–89.

101. Wood, AM, S Joseph, J Lloyd, and S Atkins. 2009. "Gratitude Influences Sleep through the Mechanism of Pre-Sleep Cognitions." *PubMed*, January. https://www.ncbi.nlm.nih.gov/pubmed/19073292.

102. P, E., Tracy A. Steen, Nansook Park, and Christopher Peterson. 2005. "Positive Psychology Progress: Empirical Validation of Interventions." *American Psychologist* 60 (5): 410–21. doi:10.1037/0003-066X.60.5.410.

103. Khazan, Olga. 2015. "The Power of 'Good Enough.'" *The Atlantic*, March 10. https://www.theatlantic.com/health/archive/2015/03/the-power-of-good-enough/387388/.

104. Krause, Neal. 2009. "Religious Involvement, Gratitude, and Change in Depressive Symptoms Over Time." *The International Journal for the Psychology of Religion* 19 (3): 155–72. doi:10.1080/10508610902880204.

105. Barnes, Robert G. 1997. *Ready for Responsibility: How to Equip Your Children for Work and Marriage*. Grand Rapids, MI: ZondervanPublishingHouse.

106. Mandell, Lewis. 2008. "The Financial Literacy of Young American Adults: Results of the 2008 National Jump$tart Coalition Survey of High School Seniors and College Students." http://www.jumpstart.org/assets/files/2008SurveyBook.pdf.

107. Grant, Kelli. 2014. "What Nation Has the Most Money-Smart Teens? It's Not the US." *CNBC*. July 9. http://www.cnbc.com/2014/07/08/teen-financial-literacy-test-country-with-most-money-smarts-not-the-us.html.

108. "Age at Which Americans Become Christian." 2017. Accessed May 11. https://home.snu.edu/~hculbert/ages.htm.

109. Street, 1615 L., NW, Suite 800 Washington, and DC 20036 202 419 4300 | Main 202 419 4349 | Fax 202 419 4372 | Media Inquiries. 2010. "Religion Among the Millennials." *Pew Research Center's Religion & Public Life Project*. February 17. http://www.pewforum.org/2010/02/17/religion-among-the-millennials/.

110. Street, 1615 L., NW, Suite 800 Washington, and DC 20036 202 419 4300 | Main 202 419 4349 | Fax 202 419 4372 | Media Inquiries. 2016. "Choosing a New Church or House of Worship." *Pew Research Center's Religion & Public Life Project*. August 23. http://www.pewforum.org/2016/08/23/choosing-a-new-church-or-house-of-worship/.

111. Bisset, Tom. 1992. *Why Christian Kids Leave the Faith*. Grand Rapids, MI: Discovery House Publishers.

112. Gross, Neil, and Simmons, Solon. 2007. "How Religious Are America's College and University Professors?" http://religion.ssrc.org/reforum/Gross_Simmons.pdf.

113. Powell, Kara E., Chap Clark, John Ortberg, and Jim Candy. 2011. *Sticky Faith: Everyday Ideas to Build Lasting Faith in Your Kids.* 8/29/11 edition. Grand Rapids, Mich: Zondervan.

114. Wright, Bradley R. E. 2010. *Christians Are Hate-Filled Hypocrites...and Other Lies You've Been Told: A Sociologist Shatters Myths From the Secular and Christian Media.* Minneapolis, Minn: Bethany House Publishers.

115. Gregston, Mark. 2008. *Dealing with Today's Teens: A Seminar for Parents and Youth Workers Workbook.* Hallsville, TX: Heartlight Ministries Foundation.

116. Powell, Kara E., Chap Clark, John Ortberg, and Jim Candy. 2011. *Sticky Faith: Everyday Ideas to Build Lasting Faith in Your Kids.* 8/29/11 edition. Grand Rapids, Mich: Zondervan.

117. Wright, Bradley R. E. 2010. *Christians Are Hate-Filled Hypocrites...and Other Lies You've Been Told: A Sociologist Shatters Myths From the Secular and Christian Media.* Minneapolis, Minn: Bethany House Publishers.

118. "Definition of BLESSING." 2017. Accessed May 11. https://www.merriam-webster.com/dictionary/blessing.

119. Trent, John, and Gary Smalley. 2011. *The Blessing: Giving the Gift of Unconditional Love and Acceptance.* Rev. and updated by John Trent. Nashville, Tenn: Thomas Nelson.

120. Matthew 12:35 NIV

121. Grandin, Temple. 2017. *The World Needs All Kinds of Minds.* Accessed May 11. https://www.ted.com/talks/temple_grandin_the_world_needs_all_kinds_of_minds.

122. Yancey, Philip. 2002. *What's So Amazing About Grace?* Revised ed. edition. Grand Rapids, Mich.: Zondervan.

123. Lucado, Max. 1997. *You Are Special.* Wheaton, Ill: Crossway.

124. Trent, John, and Judith DuFour Love. 2011. *I'd Choose You!* Nashville, Tenn: Tommy Nelson. http://www.theblessing.com/html/.

125. Scripture quotations marked (NIV) are taken from the Holy Bible, New International Version®, NIV®. Copyright © 1973, 1978, 1984, 2011 by Biblica, Inc.™ Used by permission of Zondervan. All rights reserved worldwide. www.zondervan.com The "NIV" and "New International Version" are trademarks registered in the United States Patent and Trademark Office by Biblica, Inc.™